LIFE WITH FATHER

VINNIE

" Well, this afternoon May Lewis's mother is giving a party for everyone in May's dancing class. Harlan's going to that."

CLARENCE DAY'S

LIFE WITH FATHER

MADE INTO A

P L A Y

BY

HOWARD LINDSAY

AND

RUSSEL CROUSE

WITH AN INTRODUCTION BY

BROOKS ATKINSON

1940   *Alfred A. Knopf*   NEW YORK

FEB 1 4 1940

Copyright 1939, 1940 by Howard Lindsay, Russel Crouse
and Katharine B. Day

FIRST EDITION

Manufactured in the United States of America
Published simultaneously in Canada by The Ryerson Press

*This play is not at present released for the use of non-professional
groups. When it is released, the non-professional rights will be con-
trolled exclusively by the Dramatists Play Service, 6 East 39th Street,
New York, N. Y., without whose permission in writing no performance
may be given.*

To OSCAR SERLIN *who started as our producer and remains our friend*

INTRODUCTION

BY

BROOKS ATKINSON

ALTHOUGH everyone hoped that Clarence Day's sketches of his despotic parent would make a good play, no one imagined that it would be as funny as the period comedy Howard Lindsay and Russel Crouse have written. Without vulgarizing the tartly satiric point of view they have translated Mr. Day's material into an immensely popular comedy that reminds most Americans of home. Father is now one of the representative American figures.

When Mr. Day started idly to scribble about him almost twenty years ago, no one foresaw the place Father would eventually hold in current literature and on the stage. From scattered magazine papers he grew into two books that have had a wide reading, *Life with Father* and *God and My Father*, and he does considerable roaring in *Life with Mother*. Now he presides tyrannically over the most popular comedy of a Broadway season, and will doubtless bully his stage family here and there for a long time to come. Everything about Father is very much alive today. Although Clarence Day died in 1935, that fact is hard to remember in any discussion of his domestic saga, for the humor is sly, the tone is gay, and the character is dynamic.

Good as the books are, the play has certain advantages. For the theater is concrete, vivid, and magnetic. When it says something well, it leaves an indelible impression. Since Mr. Day had no plan in mind when he began to write about his father and, in fact, never considered himself a professional writer until the public insisted that he was, he sketched his portrait at random in a number of impish bits that are casually related. But a play has to have some sort of form for the purposes of intelligible dramatic statement, and that is the major contribution Mr. Lindsay and Mr. Crouse have made to the original material. They have taken an incident here, a hint there, and a few sequences of dialogue, although there is very little dialogue in the books; and they have applied their imaginations to some of the more shadowy characters in the Day sketches. The result is a comedy that conveys Father's character as trenchantly as he could have wished, and puts him at the center of a picaresque chronicle that is rounded, logical and warm.

Obviously, Father is an individual. In point of fact he was a person, very much so — Clarence Day's parent. Fortunately he also lived long enough to read some of the first sketches and to comment vigorously, and without self-consciousness, on the accuracy of the incidents related. Although some people at first questioned the taste of such intimate family revelations, Father did not; it all seemed natural enough to him. Although Father was and is an individual, the minute the character of Father appeared on the stage in Mr. Lindsay's savory acting, everyone perceived that, willy-nilly, he had acquired universal characteristics. His family problems and his attitude toward them became the familiar experience of most fathers in the home.

Father's voice is more commanding than most male voices in the home, and his mode of action is more direct. But apart from that he represents the ludicrous impossibility of bossing a household. (Father is logical from an unreasonable point of view.) He plans the life of his wife and boys in terms of his own peace of mind — the dominant male always two jumps behind the scattered interests of his wife and the normal giddiness of four growing boys. What Father wants is simple. He wants today to be as pleasant as he remembers that yesterday was. "More of the same" is his formula for the good life — breakfast at the same hour with the bacon done to the same turn of crispness, no interruptions from the outside, dinner at home with every member of the family in his allotted place.

As for the domestic economy, Father's requirements are equally simple. He wants to know where his money is going. In the back of his head he has a budget that will look after the family necessities for the next several months and he wants every item to fall neatly into place. He is a business man; running the financial department of a family is perpetual amortization as far as he is concerned. Father is a rational person. But family life does not respond to logic. It is founded on love, which is the most distracting force God ever invented, and that is the cream of this jest. In spite of the utmost good will between members of the family, things are always getting out of hand and disturbing the even tenor of Father's expectations. Life will not conform to Father's excellent plans of it.

Before Clarence Day died, theater and screen people were asking his consent to stage and motion-picture versions of his sketches. Since the stage and screen were a little outside his experience, he never arrived at a decision. After his death it was even more difficult for his wife to decide what to do, for family loyalties and living people were involved. In the wrong hands Father and the Day family might easily turn up as buffoons in a cheapjack cartoon. What had character in the sketches might be comic-strip skulduggery in an obtuse play. That would have been unpardonable. Although Father Day had volume he also had taste. In the first book of sketches Clarence Day remarked that he was astonished and a little alarmed by the life of other families when as a college boy he began to visit his chums: "In our household things got pretty rough at times but at least we had no black gloom. Our home life was stormy but spirited. It had tang. When Father was unhappy he said so. . . . If he had ever had any meannesses in him, he might have tried to repress them. But he was a thoroughly good-hearted, warm-blooded man, and he saw no reason for hiding his feelings. They were too strong to hide anyway."

Nothing is more creditable to Mr. Lindsay and Mr. Crouse than the skill with which they have evoked out of the comic whirlwind the good will and affection of a well-bred family. The theater dotes on slapstick; both Mr. Lindsay and Mr. Crouse have proved in their musical comedies that they can handle the slapstick ably. But they are also gentlemen of taste, and they have preserved Father's dignity as a human being and the good manners of his family. Almost anybody would like to live in a family as wholesome, healthy, and alive as the one they have conjured into being on the stage.

As it happens, Father is defeated in nearly every issue that is raised. But there is no malice or cunning at work against him, and probably his wife and his boys would resent any suggestion that Father was not always having his way. For he is the backbone and jawbone of the family — a heroic figure rising grandly above the domestic scene. Mr. Lindsay has not only helped to write the character that way, but he plays it with the same passionate rectitude; and his wife, Dorothy Stickney, plays the part of Mother with fervent sincerity. People will remember *Life with Father* with amusement and gratitude all their lives, for the character forcefully represents a common family joke. Clarence Day wrote it. And now two other comic minds have also relished the humor of it.

LIFE WITH FATHER

was produced by OSCAR SERLIN at the

Empire Theatre

New York City, on the night of Nov. 8, 1939
with the following Cast:

ANNIE	played by	Katherine Bard
VINNIE	" "	Dorothy Stickney
CLARENCE	" "	John Drew Devereaux
JOHN	" "	Richard Simon
WHITNEY	" "	Raymond Roe
HARLAN	" "	Larry Robinson
FATHER	" "	Howard Lindsay
MARGARET	" "	Dorothy Bernard
CORA	" "	Ruth Hammond
MARY	" "	Teresa Wright
THE REVER^ND DR. LLOYD	—	Richard Sterling
DELIA	" "	Portia Morrow
NORA	" "	Nellie Burt
DR. HUMPHREYS	" "	A. H. Van Buren
DR. SOMERS	" "	John C. King
MAGGIE	" "	Timothy Kearse

STAGED BY *Bretaigne Windust*
SETTING & COSTUMES BY *Stewart Chaney*

Synopsis of

S C E N E S

The time: late in the 1880's.
The entire action takes place in the Morning Room
of the Day home on Madison Avenue.

A C T   I

Scene 1   *Breakfast time. An early summer morning.*
Scene 2   *Tea time. The same day.*

A C T   I I

Scene 1   *Sunday, after church. A week later.*
Scene 2   *Breakfast time. Two days later.*
          [During Scene 2 the curtain
          is lowered to denote a lapse
          of three hours.]

A C T   I I I

Scene 1   *Mid-afternoon. A month later.*
Scene 2   *Breakfast time. The next morning.*

CAST OF

CHARACTERS

FATHER	*about* 50
MOTHER (*Vinnie*)	*about* 40
CLARENCE	*about* 17
JOHN	*about* 15
WHITNEY	*about* 13
HARLAN	*about* 6
CORA (*Vinnie's Cousin*)	*about* 30
MARY SKINNER	*about* 16
THE REVEREND DR. LLOYD	*about* 50
DR. HUMPHREYS	*about* 55
DR. SOMERS	*about* 60
MARGARET, *the cook*	*about* 45
ANNIE, *a maid*	*about* 20
DELIA, *a maid*	*about* 25
NORA, *a maid*	*about* 40
MAGGIE, *a maid*	*about* 30

LIFE WITH FATHER

ACT I

A C T   I

SCENE I

The Morning Room of the Day home at 420 Madison Avenue. In the custom of the Victorian period, this was the room where the family gathered for breakfast, and because it was often the most comfortable room in the house, it served also as a living-room for the family and their intimates.

There is a large arch in the center of the upstage wall of the room, through which we can see the hall and the stairs leading to the second floor, and below them the rail of the stairwell leading to the basement. The room can be closed off from the hall by sliding doors in the archway. The front door of the house, which is stage right, can't be seen, but frequently is heard to slam.

In the Morning Room the sunshine streams through the large window at the right which looks out on Madison Avenue. The room itself is furnished with the somewhat less than comfortable furniture of the period, which is the late 1880's. The general color scheme in drapes and upholstery is green. Below the window is a large comfortable chair where Father generally sits to read his paper. Right of center is the table which serves as a living-room table, with its proper table cover and fruit bowl; but now, expanded by extra leaves, it is doing service as a breakfast table. Against the back wall, either side of the arch, are two console tables which are used by the maid as serving tables. Left of center is a sofa, with a table just above its right end holding a lamp, framed photographs, and other ornaments. In the left wall is a fireplace, its mantel draped with a lambrequin. On the mantel are a clock and other ornaments, and above the mantel is a large mirror in a Victorian frame. The room is cluttered with the minutiæ of the period, including the inevitable rubber plant, and looking down from the walls are the Day ancestors in painted portraits. The room has the warm quality that comes only from having been lived in by a family which enjoys each other's company —a family of considerable means.

As the curtain rises, ANNIE, *the new maid, a young Irish girl, is finishing setting the table for breakfast. After an uncertain look at the result she crosses over to her tray on the console table.* VINNIE *comes down the stairs and into the room.* VINNIE *is a charming, lovable, and spirited woman of forty. She has a lively mind which darts quickly away from any practical matter. She has red hair.*

ANNIE

Good morning, ma'am.

VINNIE

Good morning, Annie. How are you getting along?

ANNIE

All right, ma'am, I hope.

VINNIE

Now, don't be worried just because this is your first day. Everything's going to be all right — but I do hope nothing goes wrong. [*goes to the table.*] Now, let's see, is the table all set? [ANNIE *follows her.*] The cream and the sugar go down at this end.

ANNIE

[*placing them where* VINNIE *has indicated*] I thought in the center, ma'am; everyone could reach them easier.

VINNIE

Mr. Day sits here.

ANNIE

[*gets a tray of napkins, neatly rolled and in their rings, from the console table.*] I didn't know where to place the napkins, ma'am.

VINNIE

You can tell which go where by the rings. [*takes them from the tray and puts them down as she goes around the table.* ANNIE *follows her.*] This one belongs to Whitney — it has his initial on it, "W"; that one with the little dog on it is Harlan's, of course. He's the baby. This "J" is for John and the "C" is for Clarence. This narrow plain one is mine. And this is Mr. Day's. It's just like mine — except that it got bent one morning. And that reminds me — always be sure Mr. Day's coffee is piping hot.

ANNIE

Ah, your man has coffee instead of tea of a morning?

VINNIE

We all have coffee except the two youngest boys. They have their milk. And, Annie, always speak of my husband as Mr. Day.

ANNIE

I will that.

VINNIE

[*correcting her*] "Yes, ma'am," Annie.

ANNIE

Yes, ma'am.

VINNIE

And if Mr. Day speaks to you, just say: "Yes, sir." Don't be nervous — you'll get used to him.

[CLARENCE, *the eldest son, about seventeen, comes down the stairs and into the room. He is a manly, serious, good-looking boy. Because he is starting in at Yale next year, he thinks he is grown-up. He is red-headed.*]

CLARENCE

Good morning, Mother. [*he kisses her.*]

VINNIE

Good morning, Clarence.

CLARENCE

Did you sleep well, Mother?

VINNIE

Yes, thank you, dear.

[CLARENCE *goes to* FATHER's *chair and picks up the morning paper.*]

[*to* ANNIE] We always start with fruit, except the two young boys, who have porridge. [ANNIE *brings the fruit and porridge to the table.* CLARENCE, *looking at the paper, makes a whistling sound.*]

CLARENCE

Jiminy! Another wreck on the New Haven. That always disturbs the market. Father won't like that.

VINNIE

I do wish that New Haven would stop having wrecks. If they knew how it upset your father — [*sees that* CLARENCE'S *coat has been torn and mended.*] My soul and body, Clarence, what's happened to your coat?

CLARENCE

I tore it. Margaret mended it for me.

VINNIE

It looks terrible. Why don't you wear your blue suit?

CLARENCE

That looks worse than this one. You know, I burnt that hole in it.

VINNIE

Oh, yes — well, you can't go around looking like that. I'll have to speak to your father. Oh, dear!

[J O H N, *who is about fifteen, comes down the stairs and into the room.* J O H N *is gangly and a little overgrown. He is red-headed.*]

JOHN

Good morning, Mother. [*he kisses her.*]

VINNIE

Good morning, John.

JOHN

[*to* CLARENCE] Who won?

CLARENCE

I haven't looked yet.

JOHN

Let me see. [*he tries to take the paper away from* CLARENCE.]

CLARENCE

Be careful!

VINNIE

Boys, don't wrinkle that paper before your father's looked at it.

CLARENCE

[*to* JOHN] Yes!

[VINNIE *turns to* ANNIE.]

VINNIE

You'd better get things started. We want everything ready when Mr. Day comes down. [ANNIE *exits.*] Clarence, right after breakfast I want you and John to move the small bureau from my room into yours.

CLARENCE

What for? Is somebody coming to visit us?

JOHN

Who's coming?

VINNIE

I haven't said anyone was coming. And don't you say anything about it. I want it to be a surprise.

CLARENCE

Oh! Father doesn't know yet?

VINNIE

No. And I'd better speak to him about a new suit for you before he finds out he's being surprised by visitors.

[ANNIE *enters with a tray on which are two glasses of milk, which she puts at* HARLAN's *and* WHITNEY's *places at the table.*]

[WHITNEY *comes down the stairs and rushes into the room. He is about thirteen. Suiting his age, he is a lively active boy. He is red-headed.*]

WHITNEY

Morning. [*he kisses his mother quickly, then runs to* CLARENCE *and* JOHN.] Who won?

JOHN

The Giants, 7 to 3. Buck Ewing hit a home run.

WHITNEY

Let me see!

[HARLAN *comes sliding down the banister. He enters the room, runs to his mother, and kisses her.* HARLAN *is a roly-poly, lovable, good-natured youngster of six. He is red-headed.*]

VINNIE

How's your finger, darling?

HARLAN

It itches.

VINNIE

[*kissing the finger*] That's a sign it's getting better. Now don't scratch it. Sit down, boys. Get in your chair, darling.

> [*The boys move to the table and take their places.* CLARENCE *puts the newspaper beside his father's plate.* JOHN *stands waiting to place* VINNIE'S *chair when she sits.*]

Now, Annie, watch Mr. Day, and as soon as he finishes his fruit — [*leaves the admonition hanging in mid-air as the sound of* FATHER'S *voice booms from upstairs.*]

FATHER'S VOICE

Vinnie! Vinnie!

> [*All eyes turn toward the staircase.* VINNIE *rushes to the foot of the stairs, speaking as she goes.*]

VINNIE

What's the matter, Clare?

FATHER'S VOICE

Where's my necktie?

VINNIE

Which necktie?

FATHER'S VOICE

The one I gave you yesterday.

VINNIE

It isn't pressed yet. I forgot to give it to Margaret.

FATHER'S VOICE

I told you distinctly I wanted to wear that necktie today.

VINNIE

You've got plenty of neckties. Put on another one right away and come down to breakfast.

FATHER'S VOICE

Oh, damn! Damnation!

> [VINNIE *goes to her place at the table.* JOHN *places her chair for her, then sits.* WHITNEY *has started eating.*]

CLARENCE

Whitney!

VINNIE

Wait for your father, Whitney.

WHITNEY

Oh, and I'm in a hurry! John, can I borrow your glove today? I'm going to pitch.

JOHN

If I don't play myself.

WHITNEY

Look, if you need it, we're playing in that big field at
the corner of Fifty-seventh and Madison.

VINNIE

'Way up there!

WHITNEY

They're building a house on that vacant lot on Fiftieth
Street.

VINNIE

My! My! My! Here we move to Forty-eighth Street
just to get out of the city!

WHITNEY

Can't I start breakfast, Mother? I promised to be there
by eight o'clock.

VINNIE

After breakfast, Whitney, you have to study your catechism.

WHITNEY

Mother, can't I do that this afternoon?

VINNIE

Whitney, you have to learn five questions every morning before you leave the house.

WHITNEY

Aw, Mother —

VINNIE

You weren't very sure of yourself when I heard you last night.

WHITNEY

I know them now.

VINNIE

Let's see. [WHITNEY *rises and faces his mother.*] "What is your name?"

WHITNEY

Whitney Benjamin.

VINNIE

"Who gave you this name?"

WHITNEY

"My sponsors in baptism, wherein I was made a member of Christ, the child of God and an inheritor of the Kingdom of Heaven." Mother, if I hadn't been baptized wouldn't I have a name?

VINNIE

Not in the sight of the Church. "What did your sponsors then for you?"

WHITNEY

"They did promise and vow three things in my name —"

[F A T H E R *makes his appearance on the
stairway and comes down into the room.*
F A T H E R *is in his forties, distinguished
in appearance, with great charm and vi-
tality, extremely well dressed in a con-
servative way. He is red-headed.*]

FATHER

[*heartily*] Good morning, boys.

[*They rise and answer him.*]

Good morning, Vinnie. [*he goes to her and kisses her.*]
Have a good night?

VINNIE

Yes, thank you, Clare.

FATHER

Good! Sit down, boys.

[*The doorbell rings and a postman's
whistle is heard.*]

VINNIE

That's the doorbell, Annie. [A N N I E *exits.*] Clare,
that new suit looks very nice.

FATHER

Too damn tight! [*he sits in his place at the head of the
table.*] What's the matter with those fellows over in
London? I wrote them a year ago they were making
my clothes too tight!

VINNIE

You've put on a little weight, Clare.

FATHER

I weigh just the same as I always have. [*attacks his orange. The boys dive into their breakfasts.* ANNIE *enters with the mail, starts to take it to* VINNIE. FATHER *sees her.*] What's that? The mail? That goes to me.

> [ANNIE *gives the mail to* FATHER *and exits with her tray.*]

VINNIE

Well, Clarence has just managed to tear the only decent suit of clothes he has.

FATHER

[*looking through the mail*] Here's one for you, Vinnie. John, hand that to your mother. [*he passes the letter on.*]

VINNIE

Clare dear, I'm sorry, but I'm afraid Clarence is going to have to have a new suit of clothes.

FATHER

Vinnie, Clarence has to learn not to be so hard on his clothes.

CLARENCE

Father, I thought —

ACT III SCENE II

V I N N I E

" It's all right, Clare. If you don't love us enough there's nothing we can do about it."

FATHER

Clarence, when you start in Yale in the fall, I'm going to set aside a thousand dollars just to outfit you, but you'll get no new clothes this summer.

CLARENCE

Can't I have one of your old suits cut down for me?

FATHER

Every suit I own still has plenty of wear in it. I wear my clothes until they're worn out.

VINNIE

Well, if you want your clothes worn out, Clarence can wear them out much faster than you can.

CLARENCE

Yes, and, Father, you don't get a chance to wear them out. Every time you get a new batch of clothes, Mother sends the old ones to the missionary barrel. I guess I'm just as good as any old missionary.

[ANNIE *returns with a platter of bacon and eggs and a pot of coffee.*]

VINNIE

Clarence, before you compare yourself to a missionary, remember the sacrifices they make.

FATHER

[*chuckling*] I don't know, Vinnie, I think my clothes would look better on Clarence than on some Hottentot.

[*to* CLARENCE] Have that black suit of mine cut down to fit you before your mother gets her hands on it.

[ANNIE *clears the fruit.*]

CLARENCE

Thank you, Father. [*to* JOHN] One of Father's suits! Thank you, sir!

FATHER

Whitney, don't eat so fast.

WHITNEY

Well, Father, I'm going to pitch today and I promised to get there early, but before I go I have to study my catechism.

FATHER

What do you bother with that for?

VINNIE

[*with spirit*] Because if he doesn't know his catechism he can't be confirmed!

WHITNEY

[*pleading*] But I'm going to pitch today.

FATHER

Vinnie, Whitney's going to pitch today and he can be confirmed any old time.

VINNIE

Clare, sometimes it seems to me that you don't care whether your children get to Heaven or not.

FATHER

Oh, Whitney'll get to Heaven all right. [*to* WHIT-NEY] I'll be there before you are, Whitney; I'll see that you get in.

VINNIE

What makes you so sure they'll let you in?

FATHER

Well, if they don't I'll certainly raise a devil of a row.

> [ANNIE *is at* FATHER'S *side with the platter of bacon and eggs, ready to serve him, and draws back at this astounding declaration, raising the platter.*]

VINNIE

[*with shocked awe*] Clare, I do hope you'll behave when you get to Heaven.

> [FATHER *has turned to serve himself from the platter, but* ANNIE, *not yet recovered from the picture of* FATHER *raising a row at the gates of Heaven, is holding it too high for him.*]

FATHER

[*storming*] Vinnie, how many times have I asked you not to engage a maid who doesn't even know how to serve properly?

VINNIE

Clare, can't you see she's new and doing her best?

FATHER

How can I serve myself when she's holding that platter over my head?

VINNIE

Annie, why don't you hold it lower?

[ANNIE *lowers the platter.* FATHER *serves himself, but goes on talking.*]

FATHER

Where'd she come from anyway? What became of the one we had yesterday? I don't see why you can't keep a maid.

VINNIE

Oh, you don't!

FATHER

All I want is service.

[ANNIE *serves the others nervously. So far as* FATHER *is concerned, however, the storm has passed, and he turns genially to* WHITNEY.]

Whitney, when we get to Heaven we'll organize a baseball team of our own. [*the boys laugh.*]

VINNIE

It would be just like you to try to run things up there.

FATHER

Well, from all I've heard about Heaven, it seems to be a pretty unbusinesslike place. They could probably use a good man like me. [*stamps on the floor three times. It is his traditional signal to summon* MARGARET, *the cook, from the kitchen below.*]

VINNIE

What do you want Margaret for? What's wrong?

[ANNIE *has reached the sideboard and is sniffling audibly.*]

FATHER

[*distracted*] What's that damn noise?

VINNIE

Shhh — it's Annie.

FATHER

Annie? Who's Annie?

VINNIE

The maid.

[ANNIE, *seeing that she has attracted attention, hurries out into the hall where she can't be seen or heard.*]

Clare, aren't you ashamed of yourself?

FATHER

[*surprised*] What have I done now?

VINNIE

You made her cry — speaking to her the way you did.

FATHER

I never said a word to her — I was addressing myself to you.

VINNIE

I do wish you'd be more careful. It's hard enough to keep a maid — and the uniforms just fit this one.

> [MARGARET, *the cook, a small Irish-woman of about fifty, hurries into the room.*]

MARGARET

What's wanting?

FATHER

Margaret, this bacon is *good*.

> [MARGARET *beams and gestures deprecatingly.*]

It's *good*. It's done just right!

MARGARET

Yes, sir!

> [*She smiles and exits.* ANNIE *returns, recovered, and starts serving the coffee.* VINNIE *has opened her letter and glanced through it.*]

VINNIE

Clare, this letter gives me a good idea. I've decided that next winter I won't give a series of dinners.

FATHER

I should hope not.

VINNIE

I'll give a big musicale instead.

FATHER

You'll give a what?

VINNIE

A musicale.

FATHER

[*peremptorily*] Vinnie, I won't have my peaceful home turned into a Roman arena with a lot of hairy fiddlers prancing about.

VINNIE

I didn't say a word about hairy fiddlers. Mrs. Spiller has written me about this lovely young girl who will come for very little.

FATHER

What instrument does this inexpensive paragon play?

VINNIE

She doesn't play, Clare, she whistles.

FATHER

Whistles? Good God!

VINNIE

She whistles sixteen different pieces. All for twenty-five dollars.

FATHER

[*stormily*] I won't pay twenty-five dollars to any human peanut stand. [*he tastes his coffee, grimaces, and again stamps three times on the floor.*]

VINNIE

Clare, I can arrange this so it won't cost you a penny. If I invite fifty people and charge them fifty cents apiece, there's the twenty-five dollars right there!

FATHER

You can't invite people to your own house and charge them admission.

VINNIE

I can if the money's for the missionary fund.

FATHER

Then where will you get the twenty-five dollars to pay that poor girl for her whistling?

VINNIE

Now, Clare, let's not cross that bridge until we come to it.

FATHER

And if we do cross it, it will cost me twenty-five dollars. Vinnie, I'm putting my foot down about this musicale, just as I've had to put my foot down about your keeping this house full of visiting relatives. Why can't we live here by ourselves in peace and comfort?

[MARGARET *comes dashing into the room.*]

MARGARET

What's wanting?

FATHER

[*sternly*] Margaret, what is this? [*he holds up his coffee cup and points at it.*]

MARGARET

It's coffee, sir.

FATHER

It is not coffee! You couldn't possibly take water and coffee beans and arrive at that! It's slops, that's what it is — slops! Take it away! Take it away, I tell you!

[MARGARET *takes* FATHER'S *cup and dashes out.* ANNIE *starts to take* VINNIE'S *cup.*]

VINNIE

Leave my coffee there, Annie! It's perfectly all right!

[ANNIE *leaves the room.*]

FATHER

[*angrily*] It is not! I swear I can't imagine how she concocts such an atrocity. I come down to this table every morning hungry —

VINNIE

Well, if you're hungry, Clare, why aren't you eating your breakfast?

FATHER

What?

VINNIE

If you're hungry, why aren't you eating your breakfast?

FATHER

[*thrown out of bounds*] I am. [*he takes a mouthful of
bacon and munches it happily, his eyes falling on* HAR-
LAN.] Harlan, how's that finger? Come over here and
let me see it.

> [HARLAN *goes to his father's side. He
> shows his finger.*]

Well, that's healing nicely. Now don't pick that scab
or it will leave a scar, and we don't want scars on our
fingers, do we? [*he chuckles.*] I guess you'll remember
after this that cats don't like to be hugged. It's all right
to stroke them, but don't squeeze them. Now go back
and finish your oatmeal.

HARLAN

I don't like oatmeal.

FATHER

[*kindly*] It's good for you. Go back and eat it.

HARLAN

But I don't like it.

FATHER

[*quietly, but firmly*] I'll tell you what you like and what you don't like. You're not old enough to know about such things. You've no business not to like oatmeal. It's good.

HARLAN

I hate it.

FATHER

[*firmly, but not quietly*] That's enough! We won't discuss it! Eat that oatmeal at once!

> [*In contrast to* HARLAN, WHITNEY *has been eating his oatmeal at a terrific rate of speed. He pauses and puts down his spoon.*]

WHITNEY

I've finished *my* oatmeal. May I be excused?

FATHER

Yes, Whitney, you may go.

> [WHITNEY *slides off his chair and hurries to the stairs.*]

Pitch a good game.

VINNIE

Whitney!

WHITNEY

I'm going upstairs to study my catechism.

VINNIE

Oh, that's all right. Run along.

WHITNEY

[*on the way up*] Harlan, you'd better hurry up and finish your oatmeal if you want to go with me.

> [*Throughout breakfast* FATHER *has been opening and glancing through his mail. He has just reached one letter, however, that bewilders him.*]

FATHER

I don't understand why I'm always getting damn fool letters like this!

VINNIE

What is it, Clare?

FATHER

"Dear Friend Day: We are assigning you the exclusive rights for Staten Island for selling the Gem Home Popper for popcorn—"

CLARENCE

I think that's for me, Father.

FATHER

Then why isn't it addressed to Clarence Day, Jr.? [*he looks at the envelope.*] Oh, it is. Well, I'm sorry. I didn't mean to open your mail.

> [MARGARET *returns and slips a cup of coffee to the table beside* FATHER.]

VINNIE

I wouldn't get mixed up in that, Clarence. People like popcorn, but they won't go all the way to Staten Island to buy it.

> [FATHER *has picked up the paper and is reading it. He drinks his coffee absentmindedly.*]

FATHER

Chauncey Depew's having another birthday.

VINNIE

How nice.

FATHER

He's always having birthdays. Two or three a year. Damn! Another wreck on the New Haven!

VINNIE

Yes. Oh, that reminds me. Mrs. Bailey dropped in yesterday.

FATHER

Was she in the wreck?

VINNIE

No. But she was born in New Haven. Clarence, you're having tea with Edith Bailey Thursday afternoon.

CLARENCE

Oh, Mother, do I have to?

JOHN

[*singing*] " I like coffee, I like tea. I like the girls and the girls like me."

CLARENCE

Well, the girls don't like me and I don't like them.

VINNIE

Edith Bailey's a very nice girl, isn't she, Clare?

FATHER

Edith Bailey? Don't like her. Don't blame Clarence.

> [FATHER *goes to his chair by the window and sits down with his newspaper and a cigar. The others rise.* HARLAN *runs upstairs.* ANNIE *starts clearing the table and exits with the tray of dishes a little later.* VINNIE *speaks in a guarded tone to the two boys.*]

VINNIE

Clarence, you and John go upstairs and do — what I asked you to.

JOHN

You said the small bureau, Mother?

VINNIE

Shh! Run along.

> [*The boys go upstairs, somewhat unwillingly.* MARGARET *enters.*]

MARGARET

If you please, ma'am, there's a package been delivered with a dollar due on it. Some kitchen knives.

VINNIE

Oh, yes, those knives from Lewis & Conger's. [*she gets her purse from the drawer in the console table and gives* MARGARET *a dollar.*] Here, give this dollar to the man, Margaret.

FATHER

Make a memorandum of that, Vinnie. One dollar and whatever it was for.

VINNIE

[*looking into purse*] Clare, dear, I'm afraid I'm going to need some more money.

FATHER

What for?

VINNIE

You were complaining of the coffee this morning. Well, that nice French drip coffee pot is broken — and you know how it got broken.

FATHER

[*taking out his wallet*] Never mind that, Vinnie. As I remember, that coffee pot cost five dollars and something. Here's six dollars. [*he gives her six dollars.*] And when you get it, enter the exact amount in the ledger downstairs.

VINNIE

Thank you, Clare.

FATHER

We can't go on month after month having the household accounts in such a mess.

VINNIE

[*she sits on the arm of* FATHER's *chair*.] No, and I've thought of a system that will make my bookkeeping perfect.

FATHER

I'm certainly relieved to hear that. What is it?

VINNIE

Well, Clare dear, you never make half the fuss over how much I've spent as you do over my not being able to remember what I've spent it for.

FATHER

Exactly. This house must be run on a business basis. That's why I insist on your keeping books.

VINNIE

That's the whole point, Clare. All we have to do is open charge accounts everywhere and the stores will do my bookkeeping for me.

FATHER

Wait a minute, Vinnie —

VINNIE

Then when the bills come in you'd know exactly where your money had gone.

FATHER

I certainly would. Vinnie, I get enough bills as it is.

VINNIE

Yes, and those bills always help. They show you just where I spent the money. Now if we had charge accounts everywhere —

FATHER

Now, Vinnie, I don't know about that.

VINNIE

Clare dear, don't you hate those arguments we have every month? I certainly do. Not to have those I should think would be worth something to you.

FATHER

Well, I'll open an account at Lewis & Conger's — and one at McCreery's to start with — we'll see how it works out.

> [*He shakes his head doubtfully. Her victory gained,* VINNIE *moves away.*]

VINNIE

Thank you, Clare. Oh — the rector's coming to tea today.

FATHER

The rector? I'm glad you warned me. I'll go to the club. Don't expect me home until dinner time.

VINNIE

I do wish you'd take a little more interest in the church. [*goes behind* FATHER'S *chair and looks down at him with concern.*]

FATHER

Vinnie, getting me into Heaven's your job. If there's anything wrong with my ticket when I get there, you can fix it up. Everybody loves you so much — I'm sure God must, too.

VINNIE

I'll do my best, Clare. It wouldn't be Heaven without you.

FATHER

If you're there, Vinnie, I'll manage to get in some way, even if I have to climb the fence.

JOHN

[*from upstairs*] Mother, we've moved it. Is there anything else?

FATHER

What's being moved?

VINNIE

Never mind, Clare. I'll come right up, John. [*she goes to the arch, stops. Looks back at* FATHER.] Oh, Clare, it's eight thirty. You don't want to be late at the office.

FATHER

Plenty of time.

> [VINNIE *looks nervously toward the door, then goes upstairs.* FATHER *returns to his newspaper.* VINNIE *has barely disappeared when something in the paper arouses* FATHER'S *indignation.*]

Oh, God!

> [VINNIE *comes running downstairs.*]

VINNIE

What's the matter, Clare? What's wrong?

FATHER

Why did God make so many damn fools and Democrats?

VINNIE

[*relieved*] Oh, politics. [*she goes upstairs again.*]

FATHER

[*shouting after her*] Yes, but it's taking the bread out of our mouths. It's robbery, that's what it is, highway robbery! Honest Hugh Grant! Honest! Bah! A fine mayor you've turned out to be.

> [FATHER *launches into a vigorous denunciation of Mayor Hugh Grant, addressing that gentleman as though he were present in the room, called upon the*

> *Day carpet to listen to* FATHER'S *opin-*
> *ion of Tammany's latest attack on his*
> *pocketbook.*]

If you can't run this city without raising taxes every five minutes, you'd better get out and let someone who can. Let me tell you, sir, that the real-estate owners of New York City are not going to tolerate these conditions any longer. Tell me this — are these increased taxes going into public improvements or are they going into graft — answer me that, honestly, if you can, Mr. Honest Hugh Grant. You can't! I thought so. Bah!

> [ANNIE *enters with her tray. Hearing*
> FATHER *talking, she curtsies and backs*
> *into the hall, as if uncertain whether to*
> *intrude on* FATHER *and the Mayor.*
> VINNIE *comes downstairs.*]

If you don't stop your plundering of the pocketbooks of the good citizens of New York, we're going to throw you and your boodle Board of Aldermen out of office.

VINNIE

Annie, why aren't you clearing the table?

ANNIE

Mr. Day's got a visitor.

FATHER

I'm warning you for the last time.

VINNIE

Oh, nonsense, he's just reading his paper, Annie. Clear the table.

> [VINNIE *goes off through the arch.* ANNIE *comes in timidly and starts to clear the table.*]

FATHER

[*still lecturing Mayor Grant*] We pay you a good round sum to watch after our interests, and all we get is inefficiency!

> [ANNIE *looks around trying to see the Mayor and, finding the room empty, assumes* FATHER'S *remarks are directed at her.*]

I know you're a nincompoop and I strongly suspect you of being a scalawag.

> [ANNIE *stands petrified.* WHITNEY *comes downstairs.*]

It's graft — that's what it is — Tammany graft — and if you're not getting it, somebody else is.

WHITNEY

[*to* FATHER] Where's John? Do you know where John is?

FATHER

Dick Croker's running this town and you're just his cat's-paw.

[VINNIE *comes in from downstairs, and*
HARLAN *comes down from upstairs.*
FATHER *goes on talking. The others
carry on their conversation simultaneously, ignoring* FATHER *and his imagi-
nary visitor.*]

HARLAN

Mother, where's John?

VINNIE

He's upstairs, dear.

FATHER

And as for you, Richard Croker — don't think, just because you're hiding behind these minions you've put in
public office, that you're going to escape your legal responsibilities.

WHITNEY

[*calling upstairs*] John, I'm going to take your glove!

JOHN

[*from upstairs*] Don't you lose it! And don't let anybody else have it either!

VINNIE

Annie, you should have cleared the table long ago.

[ANNIE *loads her tray feverishly, eager
to escape.*]

FATHER

[*rising and slamming down the paper in his chair*] *Legal* responsibilities — by gad, sir, I mean *criminal* responsibilities.

[*The boys start toward the front door.*]

VINNIE

[*starting upstairs*] Now you watch Harlan, Whitney. Don't let him be anywhere the ball can hit him. Do what Whitney says, Harlan. And don't be late for lunch.

[FATHER *has reached the arch on his way out of the room, where he pauses for a final shot at Mayor Grant.*]

FATHER

Don't forget what happened to William Marcy Tweed — and if you put our taxes up once more, we'll put you in jail!

[*He goes out of the archway to the left. A few seconds later he is seen passing the arch toward the outer door wearing his square derby and carrying his stick and gloves. The door is heard to slam loudly.*]

[ANNIE *seizes her tray of dishes and runs out of the arch to the left toward the basement stairs. A second later there*

is a scream from ANNIE *and a tremen-
dous crash.*]

[JOHN *and* CLARENCE *come rushing
down and look over the rail of the stairs
below.* VINNIE *follows them almost immediately.*]

VINNIE

What is it? What happened?

CLARENCE

The maid fell downstairs.

VINNIE

I don't wonder, with your Father getting her so upset.
Why couldn't she have finished with the table before she
fell downstairs?

JOHN

I don't think she hurt herself.

VINNIE

And today of all days! Boys, will you finish the table?
And, Clarence, don't leave the house until I talk to you.
[*she goes downstairs.*]

[*During the following scene* CLAR-
ENCE *and* JOHN *remove* VINNIE'S
*best breakfast tablecloth and cram it
carelessly into the drawer of the console
table, then take out the extra leaves from*

*the table, push it together, and replace
the living-room table cover and the bowl
of fruit.*]

JOHN

What do you suppose Mother wants to talk to you
about?

CLARENCE

Oh, probably about Edith Bailey.

JOHN

What do you talk about when you have tea alone with
a girl?

CLARENCE

We don't talk about anything. I say: 'Isn't it a nice
day?' and she says: 'Yes,' and I say: 'I think it's a little
warmer than yesterday,' and she says: 'Yes, I like warm
weather, don't you?' and I say: 'Yes,' and then we wait
for the tea to come in. And then she says: 'How many
lumps?' and I say: 'Two, thank you,' and she says:
'You must have a sweet tooth,' and I can't say: 'Yes'
and I can't say: 'No,' so we just sit there and look at
each other for half an hour. Then I say: 'Well, it's time
I was going,' and she says: 'Must you?' and I say:
'I've enjoyed seeing you very much,' and she says: 'You
must come again,' and I say 'I will,' and get out.

JOHN

[*shaking his head*] Some fellows like girls.

CLARENCE

I don't.

JOHN

And did you ever notice fellows, when they get sweet on a girl — the silly things a girl can make them do? And they don't even seem to know they're acting silly.

CLARENCE

Well, not for Yours Truly!

[VINNIE *returns from downstairs.*]

VINNIE

I declare I don't see how anyone could be so clumsy.

CLARENCE

Did she hurt herself?

VINNIE

No, she's not hurt — she's just hysterical! She doesn't make sense. Your father may have raised his voice; and if she doesn't know how to hold a platter properly, she deserved it — but I know he didn't threaten to put her in jail. Oh, well! Clarence, I want you to move your things into the front room. You'll have to sleep with the other boys for a night or two.

CLARENCE

You haven't told us who's coming.

VINNIE

[*happily*] Cousin Cora. Isn't that nice?

ACT I SCENE I

VINNIE

". . . I'll have Mr. Day take us all to Delmonico's for dinner
tonight."

CLARENCE

It's not nice for me. I can't get any sleep in there with those children.

JOHN

Wait'll Father finds out she's here! There'll be a rumpus.

VINNIE

John, don't criticize your father. He's very hospitable after he gets used to the idea.

[*The doorbell rings.* JOHN *and* VINNIE *go to the window.*]

JOHN

Yes, it's Cousin Cora. Look, there's somebody with her.

VINNIE

[*looking out*] She wrote me she was bringing a friend of hers. They're both going to stay here.

[*A limping* ANNIE *passes through the hall.*]

Finish with the room, boys.

CLARENCE

Do I have to sleep with the other boys and have tea with Edith Bailey all in the same week?

VINNIE

Yes, and you'd better take your father's suit to the tailor's right away, so it will be ready by Thursday.

[VINNIE *goes down the hall to greet* CORA *and* MARY. CLARENCE *hurries off, carrying the table leaves.*]

VINNIE'S VOICE

[*in the hall*] Cora dear —

CORA'S VOICE

Cousin Vinnie, I'm so glad to see you! This is Mary Skinner.

VINNIE'S VOICE

Ed Skinner's daughter! I'm so glad to see you. Leave your bags in the hall and come right upstairs.

[VINNIE *enters, going toward the stairs.* CORA *follows her, but, seeing* JOHN, *enters the room and goes to him.* MARY *follows* CORA *in timidly.* CORA *is an attractive country cousin of about thirty.* MARY *is a refreshingly pretty small-town girl of sixteen.*]

CORA

[*seeing John*] Well, Clarence, it's so good to see you!

VINNIE

[*coming into the room*] Oh, no, that's John.

CORA

John! Why, how you've grown! You'll be a man before your mother! [*she laughs herself at this time-worn quip.*]

John, this is Mary Skinner. [*they exchange greetings.*]
Vinnie, I have so much to tell you. We wrote you Aunt
Carrie broke her hip. That was the night Robert Ingersoll lectured. Of course she couldn't get there; and it
was a good thing for Mr. Ingersoll she didn't.

[CLARENCE *enters.*]

And Grandpa Ebbetts hasn't been at all well.

CLARENCE

How do you do, Cousin Cora? I'm glad to see you.

CORA

This can't be Clarence!

VINNIE

Yes, it is.

CORA

My goodness, every time I see you boys you've grown
another foot. Let's see — you're going to St. Paul's
now, aren't you?

CLARENCE

[*with pained dignity*] St. Paul's! I was through with
St. Paul's long ago. I'm starting in Yale this fall.

MARY

Yale!

CORA

Oh, Mary, this is Clarence — Mary Skinner.

[MARY *smiles, and* CLARENCE, *the woman-hater, nods politely and walks away.*]

This is Mary's first trip to New York. She was so excited when she saw a horse car.

VINNIE

We'll have to show Mary around. I'll tell you — I'll have Mr. Day take us all to Delmonico's for dinner tonight.

MARY

Delmonico's!

CORA

Oh, that's marvelous! Think of that, Mary — Delmonico's! And Cousin Clare's such a wonderful host.

VINNIE

I know you girls want to freshen up. So come upstairs. Clarence, I'll let the girls use your room now, and when they've finished you can move, and bring up their bags. They're out in the hall. [*starts upstairs with* CORA.] I've given you girls Clarence's room, but he didn't know about it until this morning and he hasn't moved out yet.

[VINNIE *and* CORA *disappear upstairs.*]
[MARY *follows more slowly and on the second step stops and looks back.* CLAR-

MARY

"... I never met a Yale man before."

ENCE *has gone into the hall with his back toward* MARY *and stares morosely in the direction of their luggage.*]

CLARENCE

John, get their old bags.

[JOHN *disappears toward the front door. The voices of* VINNIE *and* CORA *have trailed off into the upper reaches of the house.* CLARENCE *turns to scowl in their direction and finds himself looking full into the face of* MARY.]

MARY

Cora didn't tell me about you. I never met a Yale man before.

[*She gives him a devastating smile and with an audible whinny of girlish excitement she runs upstairs.* CLARENCE *stares after her a few seconds, then turns toward the audience with a look of "What happened to me just then?" Suddenly, however, his face breaks into a smile which indicates that, whatever has happened, he likes it.*]

CURTAIN

SCENE II

The same day. Tea time.

VINNIE *and, the* RECTOR *are having tea.* THE REVEREND DR. LLOYD *is a plump, bustling man, very good-hearted and pleasant.* VINNIE *and* DR. LLOYD *have one strong point in common: their devotion to the Church and its rituals.* VINNIE's *devotion comes from her natural piety;* DR. LLOYD's *is a little more professional.*

At rise, DR. LLOYD *is seated with a cup of tea.* VINNIE *is also seated and* WHITNEY *is standing next to her, stiffly erect in the manner of a boy reciting.* HARLAN *is seated next to his mother, watching* WHITNEY's *performance.*

WHITNEY

[*reciting*] "— to worship Him, to give Him thanks; to put my whole trust in Him, to call upon Him — " [*he hesitates.*]

VINNIE

[*prompting*] "— to honor — "

WHITNEY

"— to honor His Holy Name and His word and to serve Him truly all the days of my life."

DR. LLOYD

"What is thy duty toward thy neighbor?"

WHITNEY

Whew! [*he pulls himself together and makes a brave start.*] "My duty toward my neighbor is to love him as myself, and to do to all men as I would they should do unto me; to love, honor, and succor my father and my mother; to honor and obey —"

VINNIE

"— civil authorities."

WHITNEY

"— civil authorities. To — to — to —"

VINNIE

[*to* DR. LLOYD] He really knows it.

WHITNEY

I know most of the others.

DR. LLOYD

Well, he's done very well for so young a boy. I'm sure if he applies himself between now and Sunday I could hear him again — with the others.

VINNIE

There, Whitney, you'll have to study very hard if you want Dr. Lloyd to send your name in to Bishop Potter next Sunday. I must confess to you, Dr. Lloyd, it's really my fault. Instead of hearing Whitney say his catechism this morning I let him play baseball.

WHITNEY

We won, too; 35 to 27.

DR. LLOYD

That's splendid, my child. I'm glad your side won. But winning over your catechism is a richer and fuller victory.

WHITNEY

Can I go now?

VINNIE

Yes, darling. Thank Dr. Lloyd for hearing you and run along.

WHITNEY

Thank you, Dr. Lloyd.

DR. LLOYD

Not at all, my little man.

[WHITNEY *starts out, turns back, takes a piece of cake and runs out.*]

VINNIE

Little Harlan is very apt at learning things by heart.

HARLAN

[*scrambling to his feet*] I can spell Constantinople. Want to hear me?

[DR. LLOYD *smiles his assent.*]

ACT I SCENE II

[*Rise of curtain.*]

C-o-ennaconny — annaconny — sissaconny — tan-tan-tee — and a nople and a pople and a Constantinople!

DR. LLOYD

Very well done, my child.

VINNIE

[*handing him a cake from the tea-tray*] That's nice, darling. This is what you get for saying it so well.

[HARLAN *quickly looks at the cake and back to* DR. LLOYD.]

HARLAN

Want me to say it again for you?

VINNIE

No, darling. One cake is enough. You run along and play with Whitney.

HARLAN

I can spell "huckleberry pie."

VINNIE

Run along, dear.

[HARLAN *goes out, skipping in rhythm to his recitation.*]

HARLAN

H-a-huckle — b-a-buckle — h-a-huckle-high.   H-a-huckle — b-a-buckle — huckleberry pie!

DR. LLOYD

[*amused*] You and Mr. Day must be very proud of your children.

[VINNIE *beams.*]

I was hoping I'd find Mr. Day at home this afternoon.

VINNIE

[*evasively*] Well, he's usually home from the office by this time.

DR. LLOYD

Perhaps he's gone for a gallop in the park — it's such a fine day. He's very fond of horseback riding, I believe.

VINNIE

Oh, yes.

DR. LLOYD

Tell me — has he ever been thrown from a horse?

VINNIE

Oh, no! No horse would throw Mr. Day.

DR. LLOYD

I've wondered. I thought he might have had an accident. I notice he never kneels in church.

VINNIE

Oh, that's no accident! But I don't want you to think he doesn't pray. He does. Why, sometimes you can hear him pray all over the house. But he never kneels.

DR. LLOYD

Never kneels! Dear me! I was hoping to have the op-
portunity to tell you and Mr. Day about our plans for
the new edifice.

VINNIE

I'm so glad we're going to have a new church.

DR. LLOYD

I'm happy to announce that we're now ready to proceed.
The only thing left to do is raise the money.

VINNIE

No one should hesitate about contributing to that.

[*The front door slams.*]

DR. LLOYD

Perhaps that's Mr. Day now.

VINNIE

Oh, no, I hardly think so.

[FATHER *appears in the archway.*]
Why, it is!

FATHER

Oh, damn! I forgot.

VINNIE

Clare, you're just in time. Dr. Lloyd's here for tea.

FATHER

I'll be right in. [*he disappears the other side of the archway.*]

VINNIE

I'll send for some fresh tea. [*she goes to the bell-pull and rings for the maid.*]

DR. LLOYD

Now we can tell Mr. Day about our plans for the new edifice.

VINNIE

[*knowing her man*] After he's had his tea.

[FATHER *comes back into the room.* DR. LLOYD *rises.*]

FATHER

How are you, Dr. Lloyd?

[CLARENCE *comes down the stairs and eagerly looks around for* MARY.]

CLARENCE

Oh, it was Father.

DR. LLOYD

Very well, thank you. [*they shake hands.*]

CLARENCE

[*to* VINNIE] They're not back yet?

VINNIE

No! Clarence, no!

[CLARENCE *turns, disappointed, and goes back upstairs.*]

DR. LLOYD

It's a great pleasure to have a visit with you, Mr. Day. Except for a fleeting glimpse on the Sabbath, I don't see much of you.

> [FATHER *grunts and sits down.* DELIA, *a new maid, enters.*]

DELIA

Yes, ma'am.

VINNIE

Some fresh tea and a cup for Mr. Day.

> [DELIA *exits and* VINNIE *hurries down to the tea table to start the conversation.*]

Well, Clare, did you have a busy day at the office?

FATHER

Damn busy.

VINNIE

Clare!

FATHER

Very busy day. Tired out.

VINNIE

I've ordered some fresh tea. [*to* DR. LLOYD] Poor Clare, he must work very hard. He always comes home tired. Although how a man can get tired just sitting at his desk all day, I don't know. I suppose Wall Street is just as much a mystery to you as it is to me, Dr. Lloyd.

DR. LLOYD

No, no, it's all very clear to me. My mind often goes to the business man. The picture I'm most fond of is when I envision him at the close of the day's work. There he sits — this hard-headed man of affairs — surrounded by the ledgers that he has been studying closely and harshly for hours. I see him pausing in his toil — and by chance he raises his eyes and looks out of the window at the light in God's sky and it comes over him that money and ledgers are dross.

> [FATHER *stares at* DR. LLOYD *with some amazement.*]

He realizes that all those figures of profit and loss are without importance or consequence — vanity and dust. And I see this troubled man bow his head and with streaming eyes resolve to devote his life to far higher things.

FATHER

Well, I'll be damned!

> [*At this moment* DELIA *returns with the fresh tea for* FATHER.]

VINNIE

Here's your tea, Clare.

> [FATHER *notices the new maid.*]

FATHER

Who's this?

VINNIE

[*quietly*] The new maid.

FATHER

Where's the one we had this morning?

VINNIE

Never mind, Clare.

FATHER

The one we had this morning was prettier.

> [DELIA, *with a slight resentment, exits.*
> FATHER *attacks the tea and cakes with
> relish.*]

Vinnie, these cakes are *good.*

DR. LLOYD

Delicious!

VINNIE

Dr. Lloyd wants to tell us about the plans for the new edifice.

FATHER

The new what?

VINNIE

The new church — Clare, you knew we were planning to build a new church.

DR. LLOYD

Of course, we're going to have to raise a large sum of money.

FATHER

[*alive to the danger*] Well, personally I'm against the church hop-skipping-and-jumping all over the town. And it so happens that during the last year I've suffered heavy losses in the market — damned heavy losses —

VINNIE

Clare!

FATHER

— so any contribution I make will have to be a small one.

VINNIE

But, Clare, for so worthy a cause!

FATHER

— and if your Finance Committee thinks it's too small they can blame the rascals that are running the New Haven Railroad!

DR. LLOYD

The amount everyone is to subscribe has already been decided.

FATHER

[*bristling*] Who decided it?

DR. LLOYD

After considerable thought we've found a formula which we believe is fair and equitable. It apportions the burden lightly on those least able to carry it and justly on those whose shoulders we know are stronger. We've voted that our supporting members should each contribute a sum equal to the cost of their pews.

[FATHER'S *jaw drops.*]

FATHER

I paid five thousand dollars for my pew!

VINNIE

Yes, Clare. That makes our contribution five thousand dollars.

FATHER

That's robbery! Do you know what that pew is worth today? Three thousand dollars. That's what the last one sold for. I've taken a dead loss of two thousand dollars on that pew already. Frank Baggs sold me that pew when the market was at its peak. He knew when to get out. [*he turns to* VINNIE.] And I'm warning you now that if the market ever goes up I'm going to unload that pew.

VINNIE

Clarence Day! How can you speak of the Lord's temple as though it were something to be bought and sold on Wall Street!

FATHER

Vinnie, this is a matter of dollars and cents, and that's something you don't know anything about!

VINNIE

Your talking of religion in the terms of dollars and cents seems to me pretty close to blasphemy.

DR. LLOYD

[*soothingly*] Now, Mrs. Day, your husband is a business man and he has a practical approach toward this problem. We've had to be practical about it too — we have all the facts and figures.

FATHER

Oh, really! What's the new piece of property going to cost you?

DR. LLOYD

I think the figure I've heard mentioned is eighty-five thousand dollars — or was it a hundred and eighty-five thousand dollars?

FATHER

What's the property worth where we are now?

DR. LLOYD

Well, there's quite a difference of opinion about that.

FATHER

How much do you have to raise to build the new church?

DR. LLOYD

Now, I've seen those figures — let me see — I know it depends somewhat upon the amount of the mortgage.

FATHER

Mortgage, eh? What are the terms of the amortization?

DR. LLOYD

Amortization? That's not a word I'm familiar with.

FATHER

It all seems pretty vague and unsound to me. I certainly wouldn't let any customer of mine invest on what I've heard.

[*The doorbell rings.*]

DR. LLOYD

We've given it a great deal of thought. I don't see how you can call it vague.

[DELIA *passes along the hall toward the front door.*]

FATHER

Dr. Lloyd, you preach that some day we'll all have to answer to God.

DR. LLOYD

We shall indeed!

FATHER

Well, I hope God doesn't ask you any questions with figures in them.

[CORA'S *voice is heard in the hall, thanking* DELIA. VINNIE *goes to the arch just in time to meet* CORA *and*

MARY *as they enter, heavily laden with packages, which they put down.* FATHER *and* DR. LLOYD *rise.*]

CORA

Oh, Vinnie, what a day! We've been to every shop in town and — [*she sees* FATHER.] Cousin Clare!

FATHER

[*cordially*] Cora, what are you doing in New York?

CORA

We're just passing through on our way to Springfield.

FATHER

We?

[CLARENCE *comes downstairs into the room with eyes only for* MARY.]

VINNIE

Oh, Dr. Lloyd, this is my favorite cousin, Miss Cartwright, and her friend, Mary Skinner. [*they exchange mutual how-do-you-do's.*]

DR. LLOYD

This seems to be a family reunion. I'll just run along.

FATHER

[*promptly*] Goodbye, Dr. Lloyd.

DR. LLOYD

Goodbye, Miss Cartwright. Goodbye, Miss — er —

VINNIE

Clarence, ~~you haven't said how-do-you-do to Dr. Lloyd.~~

CLARENCE

~~Goodbye, Dr. Lloyd.~~

VINNIE

[*to* DR. LLOYD] ~~I'll go to~~ the door with you. [DR. ~~LLOYD *and* VINNIE *go out, talking.*~~]

FATHER

Cora, you're as welcome as the flowers in May! Have some tea with us. [*to* DELIA] Bring some fresh tea — and some more of those cakes.

CORA

Oh, we've had tea! We were so tired shopping we had tea downtown.

[*With a gesture* FATHER *countermands his order to* DELIA, *who removes the tea table and exits.*]

MARY

At the Fifth Avenue Hotel.

FATHER

At the Fifth Avenue Hotel, eh? Who'd you say this pretty little girl was?

CORA

She's Ed Skinner's daughter. Well, Mary, at last you've met Mr. Day. I've told Mary so much about you, Cousin Clare, that she's just been dying to meet you.

FATHER

Well, sit down! Sit down! Even if you have had tea you can stop and visit for a while. As a matter of fact, why don't you both stay to dinner?

[VINNIE *enters just in time to hear this and cuts in quickly.*]

VINNIE

That's all arranged, Clare. Cora and Mary are going to have dinner with us.

FATHER

That's fine! That's fine!

CORA

Cousin Clare, I don't know how to thank you and Vinnie for your hospitality.

MARY

Yes, Mr. Day.

FATHER

Well, you'll just have to take pot luck.

CORA

No, I mean —

[V I N N I E *speaks quickly to postpone the revelation that* F A T H E R *has house guests.*]

VINNIE

Clare, did you know the girls are going to visit Aunt Judith in Springfield for a whole month?

FATHER

That's fine. How long are you going to be in New York, Cora?

CORA

All week.

FATHER

Splendid. We'll hope to see something of you, eh, Vinnie?

[C O R A *looks bewildered and is about to speak.*]

VINNIE

Did you find anything you wanted in the shops?

CORA

Just everything.

VINNIE

I want to see what you got.

CORA

I just can't wait to show you. [*she goes coyly to* F A T H E R.] But I'm afraid some of the packages can't be opened in front of Cousin Clare.

FATHER

Shall I leave the room? [*laughs at his own joke.*]

CORA

Clarence, do you mind taking the packages up to our room — or should I say your room? [*to* FATHER] Wasn't it nice of Clarence to give up his room to us for a whole week?

FATHER

[*with a sudden drop in temperature*] Vinnie!

VINNIE

Come on, Cora, I just can't wait to see what's in those packages.

> [CORA, MARY, *and* VINNIE *start out.* CLARENCE *is gathering up the packages.*]

FATHER

[*ominously*] Vinnie, I wish to speak to you before you go upstairs.

VINNIE

I'll be down in just a minute, Clare.

FATHER

I wish to speak to you now!

> [*The girls have disappeared upstairs.*]

VINNIE

I'll be up in just a minute, Cora.

[*We hear a faint "*All right*" from up-stairs.*]

FATHER

[*his voice is low but stern.*] Are those two women en-camped in this house?

VINNIE

Now, Clare!

FATHER

[*much louder*] Answer me, Vinnie!

VINNIE

Just a minute — control yourself, Clare.

[VINNIE, *sensing the coming storm, hurries to the sliding doors.* CLAR-ENCE *has reached the hall with his packages and he, too, has recognized the danger signal and as* VINNIE *closes one door he closes the other, leaving himself out in the hall and* FATHER *and* VIN-NIE *facing each other in the room.*]

VINNIE

[*persuasively*] Now, Clare, you know you've always liked Cora.

FATHER

[*exploding*] What has that got to do with her planking herself down in my house and bringing hordes of stran-gers with her?

VINNIE

[*reproachfully*] How can you call that sweet little girl a horde of strangers?

FATHER

Why don't they go to a hotel? New York is full of hotels built for the express purpose of housing such nuisances.

VINNIE

Clare! Two girls alone in a hotel! Who knows what might happen to them?

FATHER

All right. Then put 'em on the next train. If they want to roam — the damned gypsies — lend 'em a hand! Keep 'em roaming!

VINNIE

What have we got a home for if we can't show a little hospitality?

FATHER

I didn't buy this home to show hospitality — I bought it for my own comfort!

VINNIE

Well, how much are they going to interfere with your comfort living in that little room of Clarence's?

FATHER

The trouble is, damn it, they don't live there. They live in the bathroom! Every time I want to take my bath it's

full of giggling females — washing their hair. From the
time they take, you'd think it was the Seven Sutherland
Sisters. I tell you, I won't have it! Send 'em to a hotel.
I'll pay the bill gladly, but get them out of here!

> [CLARENCE *puts his head through the
> sliding door.*]

CLARENCE

Father, I'm afraid they can hear you upstairs.

FATHER

Then keep those doors closed!

VINNIE

[*with decision*] Clarence, you open those doors — open
them all the way!

> [CLARENCE *does so.*]

VINNIE

[*to* FATHER, *lowering her voice, but maintaining her
spirit*] Now, Clare, you behave yourself! [FATHER
glares at her angrily.] They're here and they're going
to stay here.

FATHER

That's enough, Vinnie! I want no more of this argument. [*he goes to his chair by the window, muttering.*]
Damnation!

CLARENCE

[*to* VINNIE] Mother, Cousin Cora's waiting for you.

FATHER

What I don't understand is why this swarm of locusts always descends on us without any warning. [*he sits down.* VINNIE *looks at him; then, convinced of her victory, she goes upstairs.*] Damn! Damnation! Damn! [*he follows her upstairs with his eyes; he remembers he is very fond of her.*] Vinnie! Dear Vinnie! [*he remembers he is very angry at her.*] Damn!

CLARENCE

Father, can't I go along with the rest of you to Delmonico's tonight?

FATHER

What's that? Delmonico's?

CLARENCE

You're taking Mother, Cora, and Mary to Delmonico's for dinner.

FATHER

[*exploding*] Oh, God!

[*At this sound from* FATHER, VINNIE *comes flying downstairs again.*]

I won't have it. I won't have it. [FATHER *stamps angrily across the room.*]

VINNIE

[*on the way down*] Clarence, the doors!

FATHER

I won't stand it, by God! I won't stand it!

> [VINNIE *and* CLARENCE *hurriedly close the sliding doors again.*]

VINNIE

Clare! What's the matter now?

FATHER

[*with the calm of anger that has turned to ice*] Do I understand that I can't have dinner in my own home?

VINNIE

It'll do us both good to get out of this house. You need a little change. It'll make you feel better.

FATHER

I have a home to have dinner in. Any time I can't have dinner at home this house is for sale!

VINNIE

Well, you can't have dinner here tonight because it isn't ordered.

FATHER

Let me tell you I'm ready to sell this place this very minute if I can't live here in peace. And we can all go and sit under a palm tree and live on breadfruit and pickles.

VINNIE

But, Clare, Cora and Mary want to see something of New York.

FATHER

Oh, that's it! Well, that's no affair of mine! I am not a guide to Chinatown and the Bowery. [*drawing himself up, he stalks out, throwing open the sliding doors. As he reaches the foot of the stairs,* MARY *comes tripping down.*]

MARY

I love your house, Mr. Day. I could just live here forever.

[FATHER *utters a bark of disgust and continues on upstairs.* MARY *comes into the room a little wide-eyed.*]

Cora's waiting for you, Mrs. Day.

VINNIE

Oh, yes, I'll run right up. [*she goes upstairs.*]

CLARENCE

I'm glad you like our house.

MARY

Oh, yes, I like it very much. I like green.

CLARENCE

I like green myself. [*she looks up at his red hair.*]

MARY

Red's my favorite color.

[*Embarrassed,* CLARENCE *suddenly hears himself talking about something he has never thought about.*]

CLARENCE

It's an interesting thing about colors. Red's a nice color in a house, too; but outside, too much red would be bad. I mean, for instance, if all the trees and the grass were red. Outside, green is the best color.

MARY

[*impressed*] That's right! I've never thought of it that way — but when you do think of it, it's quite a thought! I'll bet you'll make your mark at Yale.

CLARENCE

[*pleased, but modest*] Oh!

[*The outer door is heard to slam.*]

MARY

My mother wants me to go to college. Do you believe in girls going to college?

CLARENCE

I guess it's all right if they want to waste that much time — before they get married, I mean.

[JOHN *comes in, bringing* The Youth's Companion.]

JOHN

Oh, hello! Look! A new *Youth's Companion*!

[*They say "Hello" to him.*]

CLARENCE

[*from a mature height*] John enjoys *The Youth's Companion.*

[JOHN *sits right down and starts to read.* CLARENCE *is worried by this.*]

John!

[JOHN *looks at him non-plussed.* CLARENCE *glances toward* MARY. JOHN *remembers his manners and stands.* CLARENCE *speaks formally to* MARY.]

Won't you sit down?

MARY

Oh, thank you!

[*She sits.* JOHN *sits down again quickly and dives back into* The Youth's Companion. CLARENCE *sits beside* MARY.]

CLARENCE

As I was saying—I think it's all right for a girl to go to college if she goes to a girls' college.

MARY

Well, Mother wants me to go to Ohio Wesleyan — because it's Methodist. [*then almost as a confession.*] You see, we're Methodists.

CLARENCE

Oh, that's too bad! I don't mean it's too bad that you're a Methodist. Anybody's got a right to be anything they want. But what I mean is — we're Episcopalians.

MARY

Yes, I know. I've known ever since I saw your minister — and his collar. [*she looks pretty sad for a minute and then her face brightens.*] Oh, I just remembered — my father was an Episcopalian. He was baptized an Episcopalian. He was an Episcopalian right up to the time he married my mother. *She* was the Methodist.

[MARY's *tone would have surprised her mother — and even* MARY, *if she had been listening.*]

CLARENCE

I'll bet your father's a nice man.

MARY

Yes, he is. He owns the livery stable.

CLARENCE

He does? Well, then you must like horses.

MARY

Oh, I love horses! [*they are happily united again in their common love of horses.*]

CLARENCE

They're my favorite animal. Father and I both think there's nothing like a horse!

[FATHER *comes down the stairs and into the room. The children all stand.*]

MARY

Oh, Mr. Day, I'm having such a lovely time here!

FATHER

Clarence is keeping you entertained, eh?

MARY

Oh, yes, sir. We've been talking about everything — colors and horses and religion.

FATHER

Oh! [*to* JOHN] Has the evening paper come yet?

JOHN

No, sir.

FATHER

What are you reading?

JOHN

The Youth's Companion, sir.

[WHITNEY *and* HARLAN *enter from the hall,* WHITNEY *carrying a small box.*]

WHITNEY

Look what we've got!

FATHER

What is it?

WHITNEY

Tiddle-dy-winks. We put our money together and bought it.

FATHER

That's a nice game. Do you know how to play it?

WHITNEY

I've played it lots of times.

HARLAN

Show me how to play it.

FATHER

Here, I'll show you. [*opens the box and arranges the glass and disks.*]

MARY

[*hopefully to* CLARENCE] Are you going out to dinner with us tonight?

CLARENCE

[*looking at* FATHER] I don't know yet — but it's beginning to look as though I might.

FATHER

It's easy, Harlan. You press down like this and snap the little fellow into the glass. Now watch me — [*he snaps it and it goes off the table.*] The table isn't quite large enough. You boys better play it on the floor.

WHITNEY

Come on, Harlan, I'll take the reds, and you take the yellows.

FATHER

John, have you practiced your piano today?

JOHN

I was going to practice this evening.

FATHER

Better do it now. Music is a delight in the home.

[JOHN *exits, passing* CORA *and* VINNIE *as they enter, coming downstairs.*]

VINNIE

Clare, what do you think Cora just told me? She and Clyde are going to be married this fall!

FATHER

Oh, you finally landed him, eh?

[*Everybody laughs.*]

Well, he's a very lucky man. Cora, being married is the only way to live.

CORA

If we can be half as happy as you and Cousin Vinnie —

VINNIE

[*who has gone to the children*] Boys, shouldn't you be playing that on the table?

WHITNEY

The table isn't big enough. Father told us to play on the floor.

VINNIE

My soul and body! Look at your hands! Delia will have your supper ready in a few minutes. Go wash your hands right away and come back and show Mother they're clean.

> [*The boys pick up the tiddle-dy-winks and depart reluctantly. From the next room we hear* JOHN *playing "The Happy Farmer."*]

FATHER

[*sitting down on the sofa with* MARY] Vinnie, this young lady looks about the same age you were when I came out to Pleasantville to rescue you.

VINNIE

Rescue me! You came out there to talk me into marrying you.

FATHER

It worked out just the same. I saved you from spending the rest of your life in that one-horse town.

VINNIE

Cora, the other day I came across a tin-type of Clare taken in Pleasantville. I want to show it to you. You'll see who needed rescuing. [*she goes to the table and starts to rummage around in its drawer.*]

FATHER

There isn't time for that, Vinnie. If we're going to Delmonico's for dinner hadn't we all better be getting ready? It's after six now.

CORA

Gracious! I'll have to start. If I'm going to dine in public with a prominent citizen like you, Cousin Clare — I'll have to look my best. [*she goes to the arch.*]

MARY

I've changed already.

CORA

Yes, I know, but I'm afraid I'll have to ask you to come along and hook me up, Mary.

MARY

Of course.

CORA

It won't take a minute and then you can come right back.

[FATHER *rises.* MARY *crosses in front
of* FATHER *and starts toward the hall,
then turns and looks back at him.*]

MARY

Mr. Day, were you always an Episcopalian?

FATHER

What?

MARY

Were you always an Episcopalian?

FATHER

I've always gone to the Episcopal church, yes.

MARY

But you weren't baptized a Methodist or anything, were
you? You were baptized an Episcopalian?

FATHER

Come to think of it, I don't believe I was ever baptized
at all.

MARY

Oh!

VINNIE

Clare, that's not very funny, joking about a subject like
that.

FATHER

I'm not joking — I remember now — I never was baptized.

VINNIE

Clare, that's ridiculous, everyone's baptized.

FATHER

[*sitting down complacently*] Well, I'm not.

VINNIE

Why, no one would keep a little baby from being baptized.

FATHER

You know Father and Mother — free-thinkers, both of them — believed their children should decide those things for themselves.

VINNIE

But, Clare —

FATHER

I remember when I was ten or twelve years old, Mother said I ought to give some thought to it. I suppose I thought about it, but I never got around to having it done to me.

> [*The shock to* VINNIE *is as great as if* FATHER *had calmly announced himself guilty of murder. She walks to* FATHER *staring at him in horror.* CORA *and* MARY, *sensing the coming battle, withdraw to the neutral shelter of the hall.*]

VINNIE

Clare, do you know what you're saying?

FATHER

I'm saying I've never been baptized.

VINNIE

[*in a sudden panic*] Then something has to be done about it right away.

FATHER

[*not the least concerned*] Now, Vinnie, don't get excited over nothing.

VINNIE

Nothing! [*then as only a woman can ask such a question*] Clare, why haven't you ever told me?

FATHER

What difference does it make?

VINNIE

[*the panic returning*] I've never heard of anyone who wasn't baptized. Even the savages in darkest Africa —

FATHER

It's all right for savages and children. But if an oversight was made in my case it's too late to correct it now.

VINNIE

But if you're not baptized you're not a Christian!

FATHER

[*rising in wrath*] Why, confound it, of course I'm a Christian! A damn good Christian, too!

> [FATHER'S *voice tells* CLARENCE *a major engagement has begun. He hurriedly springs to the sliding doors and closes them, removing himself,* MARY, *and* CORA *from the scene of action.*]

A lot better Christian than those psalm-singing donkeys in church!

VINNIE

You can't be if you won't be baptized.

FATHER

I won't be baptized and I will be a Christian! I beg to inform you I'll be a Christian in my own way.

VINNIE

Clare, don't you want to meet us all in Heaven?

FATHER

Of course! And I'm going to!

VINNIE

But you can't go to Heaven if you're not baptized!

FATHER

That's a lot of folderol!

VINNIE

Clarence Day, don't you blaspheme like that! You're coming to church with me before you go to the office in the morning and be baptized then and there!

FATHER

Vinnie, don't be ridiculous! If you think I'm going to stand there and have some minister splash water on me at my age, you're mistaken!

VINNIE

But, Clare —

FATHER

That's enough of this, Vinnie. I'm hungry. [*draws himself up and starts for the door. He does not realize that he and* VINNIE *are now engaged in a battle to the death.*] I'm dressing for dinner. [*throws open the doors, revealing* WHITNEY *and* HARLAN, *who obviously have been eavesdropping and have heard the awful revelation of* FATHER'S *paganism.* FATHER *stalks past them upstairs. The two boys come down into the room staring at their mother, who has been standing, too shocked at* FATHER'S *callous impiety to speak or move.*]

WHITNEY

Mother, if Father hasn't been baptized he hasn't any name. In the sight of the Church he hasn't any name.

VINNIE

That's right! [*to herself*] Maybe we're not even married!

[*This awful thought takes possession of* VINNIE. *Her eyes turn slowly toward the children and she suddenly realizes their doubtful status. Her hand goes to her mouth to cover a quick gasp of horror as the curtain falls.*]

CURTAIN

A C T I I

SCENE I

The same.

The following Sunday. After church.

The stage is empty as the curtain rises. VINNIE *comes into the archway from the street door, dressed in her Sunday best, carrying her prayer book, hymnal, and a cold indignation. As soon as she is in the room,* FATHER *passes across the hall in his Sunday cutaway and silk hat, carrying gloves and cane.* VINNIE *looks over her shoulder at him as he disappears.* CORA, WHITNEY, *and* HARLAN *come into the room,* CORA *glancing after* FATHER *and then toward* VINNIE. *All three walk as though the sound of a footfall might cause an explosion, and speak in subdued tones.*

HARLAN

Cousin Cora, will you play a game of tiddle-dy-winks with me before you go?

CORA

I'm going to be busy packing until it's time to leave.

WHITNEY

We can't play games on Sunday.

> [*We hear the door close and* JOHN *enters and looks into the room apprehensively.*]

CORA

John, where are Clarence and Mary?

JOHN

They dropped behind — 'way behind! [*he goes upstairs.* WHITNEY *takes* HARLAN'S *hat from him and starts toward the arch.*]

VINNIE

Whitney, don't hang up your hat. I want you to go over to Sherry's for the ice-cream for dinner. Tell Mr. Sherry strawberry — if he has it. And take Harlan with you.

WHITNEY

All right, Mother. [*he and* HARLAN, *trained in the good manners of the period, bow and exit.*]

CORA

Oh, Vinnie, I hate to leave. We've had such a lovely week.

VINNIE

[*voice quivers in a tone of scandalized apology*] Cora, what must you think of Clare, making such a scene on his way out of church today?

CORA

Cousin Clare probably thinks that you put the rector up to preaching that sermon.

VINNIE

[*tone changes from apology to self-defense with overtones of guilt*] Well, I had to go to see Dr. Lloyd to find out whether we were really married. The sermon on baptism was his own idea. If Clare just hadn't *shouted* so — now the whole congregation knows he's never been baptized! But he's going to be, Cora — you mark my words — he's going to be! I just couldn't go to Heaven without Clare. Why, I get lonesome for him when I go to Ohio.

> [FATHER *enters holding his watch. He's also holding his temper. He speaks quietly.*]

FATHER

Vinnie, I went to the dining-room and the table isn't set for dinner yet.

VINNIE

We're having dinner late today.

FATHER

Why can't I have my meals on time?

VINNIE

The girls' train leaves at one-thirty. Their cab's coming at one o'clock.

FATHER

Cab? The horse cars go right past our door.

VINNIE

They have those heavy bags.

FATHER

Clarence and John could have gone along to carry their bags. Cabs are just a waste of money. Why didn't we have an early dinner?

VINNIE

There wasn't time for an early dinner and church, too.

FATHER

As far as I'm concerned this would have been a good day to miss church.

VINNIE

[*spiritedly*] I wish we had!

FATHER

[*flaring*] I'll bet you put him up to preaching that sermon!

VINNIE

I've never been so mortified in all my life! You stamping up the aisle roaring your head off at the top of your voice!

FATHER

That Lloyd needn't preach at me as though I were some damn criminal! I wanted him to know it, and as far as I'm concerned the whole congregation can know it, too!

VINNIE

They certainly know it now!

FATHER

That suits me!

VINNIE

[*pleading*] Clare, you don't seem to understand what the church is for.

FATHER

[*laying down a new Commandment*] Vinnie, if there's one place the church should leave alone, it's a man's soul!

VINNIE

Clare, dear, don't you believe what it says in the Bible?

FATHER

A man has to use his common sense about the Bible, Vinnie, if he has any. For instance, you'd be in a pretty fix if I gave all my money to the poor.

VINNIE

Well, that's just silly!

FATHER

Speaking of money — where are this month's bills?

VINNIE

Clare, it isn't fair to go over the household accounts while you're hungry.

FATHER

Where are those bills, Vinnie?

VINNIE

They're downstairs on your desk.

> [FATHER *exits almost eagerly. Figures are something he understands better than he does women.*]

Of all times! [*to* CORA] It's awfully hard on a woman to love a man like Clare so much.

CORA

Yes, men can be aggravating. Clyde gets me so provoked! We kept company for six years, but the minute he proposed — the moment I said "Yes" — he began to take me for granted.

VINNIE

You have to expect that, Cora. I don't believe Clare has come right out and told me he loves me since we've been married. Of course I know he does, because I keep reminding him of it. You have to keep reminding them, Cora.

[*The door slams.*]

CORA

That must be Mary and Clarence. [*there's a moment's pause. The two women look toward the hall — then at each other with a knowing sort of smile.* CORA *rises, goes up to the arch, peeks out — then faces front and innocently asks:*] Is that you, Mary?

MARY

[*dashing in*] Yes!

[CLARENCE *crosses the arch to hang up his hat.*]

CORA

We have to change our clothes and finish our packing. [*goes upstairs.*]

[CLARENCE *returns as* MARY *starts up the stairs.*]

MARY

[*to* CLARENCE] It won't take me long.

CLARENCE

Can I help you pack?

VINNIE

[*shocked*] Clarence!

[MARY *runs upstairs.* CLARENCE
drifts into the living-room, somewhat
abashed. VINNIE *collects her hat and*
gloves, starts out, stops to look at CLAR-
ENCE, *then comes down to him.*]

Clarence, why didn't you kneel in church today?

CLARENCE

What, Mother?

VINNIE

Why didn't you kneel in church today?

CLARENCE

[*troubled*] I just couldn't.

VINNIE

Has it anything to do with Mary? I know she's a Methodist.

CLARENCE

Oh, no, Mother! Methodists kneel. Mary told me.
They don't get up and down so much, but they stay
down longer.

VINNIE

If it's because your father doesn't kneel — you must
remember he wasn't brought up to kneel in church. But
you were — you always have — and, Clarence, you want
to, don't you?

CLARENCE

Oh, yes! I wanted to today! I started to — you saw me
start — but I just couldn't.

VINNIE

Is that suit of your father's too tight for you?

CLARENCE

No, it's not too *tight*. It fits fine. But it *is* the suit. Very
peculiar things have happened to me since I started to
wear it. I haven't been myself since I put it on.

VINNIE

In what way, Clarence? How do you mean?

[CLARENCE *pauses, then blurts out his
problem.*]

CLARENCE

Mother, I can't seem to make these clothes do anything
Father wouldn't do!

VINNIE

That's nonsense, Clarence — and not to kneel in church
is a sacrilege.

CLARENCE

But making Father's trousers kneel seemed more of a
sacrilege.

VINNIE

Clarence!

CLARENCE

No! Remember the first time I wore this? It was at Dora Wakefield's party for Mary. Do you know what happened? We were playing musical chairs and Dora Wakefield sat down suddenly right in my lap. I jumped up so fast she almost got hurt.

VINNIE

But it was all perfectly innocent.

CLARENCE

It wasn't that Dora was sitting on my lap — she was sitting on Father's trousers. Mother, I've got to have a suit of my own. [CLARENCE's *metaphysical problem is one that* VINNIE *can't cope with at this particular minute.*]

VINNIE

My soul and body! Clarence, you have a talk with your father about it. I'm sure if you approach him the right way — you know — tactfully — he'll see —

[MARY *comes downstairs and hesitates at the arch.*]

MARY

Oh, excuse me.

VINNIE

Gracious! Have you finished your packing?

MARY

Practically. I never put my comb and brush in until I'm ready to close my bag.

VINNIE

I must see Margaret about your box lunch for the train. I'll leave you two together. Remember, it's Sunday. [*she goes downstairs.*]

CLARENCE

I was hoping we could have a few minutes together before you left.

MARY

[*not to admit her eagerness*] Cora had so much to do I wanted to get out of her way.

CLARENCE

Well, didn't you want to see me?

MARY

[*self-consciously*] I did want to tell you how much I've enjoyed our friendship.

CLARENCE

You're going to write me when you get to Springfield, aren't you?

MARY

Of course, if you write me first.

CLARENCE

But you'll have something to write about — your trip — and Aunt Judith — and how things are in Springfield. You write me as soon as you get there.

MARY

Maybe I'll be too busy. Maybe I won't have time. [*she sits on the sofa.*]

CLARENCE

[*with the authority of* FATHER'S *trousers*] You find the time! Let's not have any nonsense about that! You'll write me first — and you'll do it right away, the first day! [*sits beside her.*]

MARY

How do you know I'll take orders from you?

CLARENCE

I'll show you. [*he takes a quick glance toward the hall.*] Give me your hand!

MARY

Why should I?

CLARENCE

Give me your hand, confound it!

[MARY *gives it to him.*]

MARY

What do you want with my hand?

ACT II SCENE I

M A R Y

" What do you want with my hand? "

CLARENCE

I just wanted it. [*holding her hand, he melts a little and smiles at her. She melts, too. Their hands, clasped together, are resting on* CLARENCE'S *knee and they relax happily.*] What are you thinking about?

MARY

I was just thinking.

CLARENCE

About what?

MARY

Well, when we were talking about writing each other I was hoping you'd write me first because that would mean you liked me.

CLARENCE

[*with the logic of the male*] What's writing first got to do with my liking you?

MARY

Oh, you *do* like me?

CLARENCE

Of course I do. I like you better than any girl I ever met.

MARY

[*with the logic of the female*] But you don't like me well enough to write first?

CLARENCE

I don't see how one thing's got anything to do with the other.

MARY

But a girl can't write first — because she's a *girl*.

CLARENCE

That doesn't make sense. If a girl has something to write about and a fellow hasn't, there's no reason why she shouldn't write first.

MARY

[*starting a flanking movement*] You know, the first few days I was here you'd do anything for me and then you changed. You used to be a lot of fun — and then all of a sudden you turned into an old sober-sides.

CLARENCE

When did I?

MARY

The first time I noticed it was when we walked home from Dora Wakefield's party. My, you were on your dignity! You've been that way ever since. You even dress like an old sober-sides.

> [CLARENCE's *face changes as* FA-
> THER's *pants rise to haunt him. Then
> he notices that their clasped hands are
> resting on these very pants, and he lifts
> them off. Agony obviously is setting in.*
> MARY *sees the expression on his face.*]

What's the matter?

CLARENCE

I just happened to remember something.

MARY

What?

> [CLARENCE *doesn't answer, but his face does.*]

Oh, I know. This is the last time we'll be together. [*she puts her hand on his shoulder. He draws away.*]

CLARENCE

Mary, please!

MARY

But, Clarence! We'll see each other in a month. And we'll be writing each other, too. I hope we will. [*she gets up.*] Oh, Clarence, please write me first, because it will show me how much you like me. Please! I'll show you how much I like you! [*she throws herself on his lap and buries her head on his shoulder.* CLARENCE *stiffens in agony.*]

CLARENCE

[*hoarsely*] Get up! Get up!

> [*She pulls back her head and looks at him, then springs from his lap and runs away, covering her face and sobbing.* CLARENCE *goes to her.*]

Don't do that, Mary! Please don't do that!

MARY

Now you'll think I'm just a bold and forward girl.

CLARENCE

Oh, no!

MARY

Yes, you will — you'll think I'm bold!

CLARENCE

Oh, no — it's not that.

MARY

[*hopefully*] Was it because it's Sunday?

CLARENCE

[*in despair*] No, it would be the same any day — [*he is about to explain, but* MARY *flares.*]

MARY

Oh, it's just because you didn't want me sitting on your lap.

CLARENCE

It was nice of you to do it.

MARY

It was nice of me! So you told me to get up! You just couldn't bear to have me sit there. Well, you needn't write me first. You needn't write me any letters at all, because I'll tear them up without opening them!

[FATHER *enters the archway, a sheath of bills in his hand and his account book under his arm.*]

I guess I know now you don't like me! I never want to see you again. I — I —

> [*She breaks and starts to run toward the stairs. At the sight of* FATHER *she stops, but only for a gasp, then continues on upstairs, unable to control her sobs.* CLARENCE, *who has been standing in unhappy indecision, turns to follow her, but stops short at the sight of* FATHER, *who is standing in the arch looking at him with some amazement.* FATHER *looks from* CLARENCE *toward the vanished* MARY, *then back to* CLARENCE.]

FATHER

Clarence, that young girl is crying — she's in tears. What's the meaning of this?

CLARENCE

I'm sorry, Father, it's all my fault.

FATHER

Nonsense! What's that girl trying to do to you?

CLARENCE

What? No, she wasn't — it was — I — how long have you been here?

FATHER

Well, whatever the quarrel was about, Clarence, I'm glad you held your own. Where's your mother?

CLARENCE

[*desperately*] I have to have a new suit of clothes —
you've *got* to give me the money for it.

[FATHER's *account book reaches the
table with a sharp bang as he stares at*
CLARENCE *in astonishment.*]

FATHER

Young man, do you realize you're addressing your
father?

[CLARENCE *wilts miserably and sinks
into a chair.*]

CLARENCE

I'm sorry, Father — I apologize — but you don't know
how important this is to me. [CLARENCE's *tone of
misery gives* FATHER *pause.*]

FATHER

A suit of clothes is so — ? Now, why should a — ?
[*something dawns on* FATHER *and he looks up in the
direction in which* MARY *has disappeared, then looks
back at* CLARENCE.] Has your need for a suit of
clothes anything to do with that young lady?

CLARENCE

Yes, Father.

FATHER

Why, Clarence! [*suddenly realizes that women have
come into* CLARENCE's *emotional life and there comes*

a yearning to protect this inexperienced and defenseless member of his own sex.] This comes as quite a shock to me.

CLARENCE

What does, Father?

FATHER

Your being so grown up! Still, I might have known that if you're going to college this fall — yes, you're at an age when you'll be meeting girls. Clarence, there are things about women that I think you ought to know! [*he goes up and closes the doors, then comes down and sits beside* CLARENCE, *hesitating for a moment before he speaks.*] Yes, I think it's better for you to hear this from me than to have to learn it for yourself. Clarence, women aren't the angels that you think they are! Well, now — first, let me explain this to you. You see, Clarence, we men have to run this world and it's not an easy job. It takes work, and it takes thinking. A man has to be sure of his facts and figures. He has to reason things out. Now, you take a woman — a woman thinks — no I'm wrong right there — a woman doesn't think at all! She gets stirred up! And she gets stirred up over the damnedest things! Now, I love my wife just as much as any man, but that doesn't mean I should stand for a lot of folderol! By God! I won't stand for it! [*looks around toward the spot where he had his last clash with* VINNIE.]

CLARENCE

Stand for what, Father?

FATHER

[*to himself*] That's the one thing I will not submit myself to. [*has ceased explaining women to* CLARENCE *and is now explaining himself.*] Clarence, if a man thinks a certain thing is the wrong thing to do he shouldn't do it. If he thinks a thing is right he should do it. Now that has nothing to do with whether he loves his wife or not.

CLARENCE

Who says it has, Father?

FATHER

They do!

CLARENCE

Who, sir?

FATHER

Women! They get stirred up and then they try to get you stirred up, too. If you can keep reason and logic in the argument, a man can hold his own, of course. But if they can *switch* you — pretty soon the argument's about whether you love them or not. I swear I don't know how they do it! Don't you let 'em, Clarence! Don't you let 'em!

CLARENCE

I see what you mean so far, Father. If you don't watch yourself, love can make you do a lot of things you don't want to do.

FATHER

Exactly!

CLARENCE

But if you do watch out and know just how to handle women —

FATHER

Then you'll be all right. All a man has to do is be firm. You know how sometimes I have to be firm with your mother. Just now about this month's household accounts —

CLARENCE

Yes, but what can you do when they cry?

FATHER

[*he gives this a moment's thought.*] Well, that's quite a question. You just have to make them understand that what you're doing is for their good.

CLARENCE

I see.

FATHER

[*rising*] Now, Clarence, you know all about women. [*goes to the table and sits down in front of his account book, opening it.* CLARENCE *rises and looks at him.*]

CLARENCE

But, Father —

FATHER

Yes, Clarence.

CLARENCE

I thought you were going to tell me about —

FATHER

About what?

CLARENCE

About women.

[FATHER *realizes with some shock that* CLARENCE *expected him to be more specific.*]

FATHER

Clarence, there are some things gentlemen don't discuss! I've told you all you need to know. The thing for you to remember is — be firm!

[CLARENCE *turns away. There is a knock at the sliding doors.*]

Yes, come in.

[MARY *opens the doors.*]

MARY

Excuse me!

[MARY *enters.* FATHER *turns his attention to the household accounts.* MARY *goes to the couch and picks up*

*her handkerchief and continues around
the couch.* CLARENCE *crosses to meet
her above the couch, determined to be
firm.* MARY *passes him without a glance.*
CLARENCE *wilts, then again assuming
firmness, turns up into the arch in an at-
tempt to quail* MARY *with a look.* MARY
marches upstairs ignoring him. CLAR-
ENCE *turns back into the room defeated.
He looks down at his clothes unhappily,
then decides to be firm with his father.
He straightens up and steps toward him.
At this moment* FATHER, *staring at a
bill, emits his cry of rage.*]

FATHER

Oh, God!

[CLARENCE *retreats.* FATHER *rises
and holds the bill in question between
thumb and forefinger as though it were
too repulsive to touch.* VINNIE *comes
rushing down the stairs.*]

VINNIE

What's the matter, Clare? What's wrong?

FATHER

I will *not* send this person a check!

[VINNIE *looks at it.*]

VINNIE

Why, Clare, that's the only hat I've bought since March and it was reduced from forty dollars.

FATHER

I don't question your buying the hat or what you paid for it, but the person from whom you bought it — this Mademoiselle Mimi — isn't fit to be in the hat business or any other.

VINNIE

I never went there before, but it's a very nice place and I don't see why you object to it.

FATHER

[*exasperated*] I object to it because this confounded person doesn't put her name on her bills! Mimi what? Mimi O'Brien? Mimi Jones? Mimi Weinstein?

VINNIE

How do I know? It's just Mimi.

FATHER

It isn't just Mimi. She must have some other name, damn it! Now, I wouldn't make out a check payable to Charley or to Jimmy, and I won't make out a check payable to Mimi. Find out what her last name is, and I'll pay her the money.

VINNIE

All right. All right. [*she starts out.*]

FATHER

Just a minute, Vinnie, that isn't all.

VINNIE

But Cora will be leaving any minute, Clare, and it isn't
polite for me —

FATHER

Never mind Cora. Sit down.

[CLARENCE *goes into the hall, looks
upstairs, wanders up and down the hall
restlessly.* VINNIE *reluctantly sits
down opposite* FATHER *at the table.*]

Vinnie, you know I like to live well, and I want my family to live well. But this house must be run on a business
basis. I must know how much money I'm spending and
what for. For instance, if you recall, two weeks ago I
gave you six dollars to buy a new coffee pot —

VINNIE

Yes, because you broke the old one. You threw it right
on the floor.

FATHER

I'm not talking about that. I'm simply endeavoring·—

VINNIE

But it was so silly to break that nice coffee pot, Clare,
and there was nothing the matter with the coffee that
morning. It was made just the same as always.

FATHER

It was not! It was made in a damned barbaric manner!

VINNIE

I couldn't get another imported one. That little shop has stopped selling them. They said the tariff wouldn't let them. And that's your fault, Clare, because you're always voting to raise the tariff.

FATHER

The tariff protects America against cheap foreign labor. [*he sounds as though he is quoting.*] Now I find that —

VINNIE

The tariff does nothing but put up the prices and that's hard on everybody, especially the farmer. [*she sounds as though she is quoting back.*]

FATHER

[*annoyed*] I wish to God you wouldn't talk about matters you don't know a damn thing about!

VINNIE

I do too know about them. Miss Gulick says every intelligent woman should have some opinion —

FATHER

Who, may I ask, is Miss Gulick?

VINNIE

Why, she's that current-events woman I told you about and the tickets are a dollar every Tuesday.

FATHER

Do you mean to tell me that a pack of idle-minded females pay a dollar apiece to hear another female gabble
about the events of the day? Listen to me if you want
to know anything about the events of the day!

VINNIE

But you get so excited, Clare, and besides, Miss Gulick
says that our President, whom you're always belittling,
prays to God for guidance and —

FATHER

[*having had enough of Miss Gulick*] Vinnie, what happened to that six dollars?

VINNIE

What six dollars?

FATHER

I gave you six dollars to buy a new coffee pot and now I
find that you apparently got one at Lewis & Conger's
and charged it. Here's their bill: "One coffee pot —
five dollars."

VINNIE

So you owe me a dollar and you can hand it right over.
[*she holds out her hand for it.*]

FATHER

I'll do nothing of the kind! What did you do with that
six dollars?

VINNIE

Why, Clare, I can't tell you now, dear. Why didn't you ask me at the time?

FATHER

Oh, my God!

VINNIE

Wait a moment! I spent four dollars and a half for that new umbrella I told you I wanted and you said I didn't need, but I did, very much.

> [FATHER *takes his pencil and writes in the account book.*]

FATHER

Now we're getting somewhere. One umbrella — four dollars and a half.

VINNIE

And that must have been the week I paid Mrs. Tobin for two extra days' washing.

FATHER

[*entering the item*] Mrs. Tobin.

VINNIE

So that was two dollars more.

FATHER

Two dollars.

VINNIE

That makes six dollars and fifty cents. And <u>that</u>'s another fifty cents you owe me.

FATHER

I don't owe you anything. [*stung by* VINNIE'*s tactics
into a determination to pin her butterfly mind down.*]
What you owe me is an explanation of where my money's
gone! We're going over this account book item by item.
[*starts to sort the bills for the purposes of cross-exami-
nation, but the butterfly takes wing again.*]

VINNIE

I do the very best I can to keep down expenses. And you
know yourself that Cousin Phoebe spends twice as much
as we do.

FATHER

Damn Cousin Phoebe!— I don't wish to be told how she
throws her money around.

VINNIE

Oh, Clare, how can you? And I thought you were so
fond of Cousin Phoebe.

FATHER

All right, I am fond of Cousin Phoebe, but I can get
along without hearing so much about her.

VINNIE

You talk about your own relatives enough.

FATHER

[*hurt*] That's not fair, Vinnie. When I talk about my relatives I criticize them.

VINNIE

If I can't even speak of Cousin Phoebe —

FATHER

You can speak of her all you want to — but I won't have Cousin Phoebe or anyone else dictating to me how to run my house. Now this month's total —

VINNIE

[*righteously*] I didn't say a word about her dictating, Clare — she isn't that kind!

FATHER

[*dazed*] I don't know what you said, now. You never stick to the point. I endeavor to show you how to run this house on a business basis and you wind up by jibbering and jabbering about everything under the sun. If you'll just explain to me —

> [*Finally cornered,* VINNIE *realizes the time has come for tears. Quietly she turns them on.*]

VINNIE

I don't know what you expect of me. I tire myself out chasing up and down those stairs all day long — trying to look after your comfort — to bring up our children —

I do the mending and the marketing and as if that isn't enough, you want me to be an expert bookkeeper, too.

FATHER

[*touched where* VINNIE *has hoped to touch him*] Vinnie, I want to be reasonable; but can't you understand? —I'm doing all this for your own good.

[VINNIE *rises with a moan.* FATHER *sighs with resignation.*]

I suppose I'll have to go ahead just paying the bills and hoping I've got money enough in the bank to meet them. But it's all very discouraging.

VINNIE

I'll try to do better, Clare.

[FATHER *looks up into her tearful face and melts.*]

FATHER

That's all I'm asking.

[*She goes to him and puts her arm around his shoulder.*]

I'll go down and make out the checks and sign them.

[VINNIE *doesn't seem entirely consoled, so he attempts a lighter note to cheer her up.*]

Oh, Vinnie, maybe I haven't any right to sign those checks, since in the sight of the Lord I haven't any name at all. Do you suppose the bank will feel that way about it too — or do you think they'll take a chance? [*he should not have said this.*]

VINNIE
That's right! Clare, to make those checks good you'll have to be baptized right away.

FATHER
[*retreating angrily*] Vinnie, the bank doesn't care whether I've been baptized or not!

VINNIE
Well, I care! And no matter what Dr. Lloyd says, I'm not sure we're really married.

FATHER
Damn it, Vinnie, we have four children! If we're not married now we never will be!

VINNIE
Oh, Clare, don't you see how serious this is? You've got to do something about it.

FATHER
Well, just now I've got to do something about these damn bills you've run up. [*sternly*] I'm going downstairs.

ACT II SCENE I

FATHER

" All right. All right. All right."

(He takes out the dollar and a half from his change purse and gives it to her.)

VINNIE

Not before you give me that dollar and a half!

FATHER

What dollar and a half?

VINNIE

The dollar and a half you owe me!

FATHER

[*thoroughly enraged*] I don't owe you any dollar and a half! I gave you money to buy a coffee pot for me and somehow it turned into an umbrella for you.

VINNIE

Clarence Day, what kind of a man are you? Quibbling about a dollar and a half when your immortal soul is in danger! And what's more —

FATHER

All right. All right. All right. [*he takes the dollar and a half from his change purse and gives it to her.*]

VINNIE

[*smiling*] Thank you, Clare. [VINNIE *turns and leaves the room. Her progress upstairs is a one-woman march of triumph.*]

    [FATHER *puts his purse back, gathers up his papers and his dignity, and starts out.* CLARENCE *waylays him in the arch.*]

CLARENCE

Father — you never did tell me — can I have a new suit of clothes?

FATHER

No, Clarence! I'm sorry, but I have to be firm with you, too!

> [*He stalks off.* JOHN *comes down the stairs carrying a traveling bag, which he takes out toward the front door. He returns empty-handed and starts up the stairs again.*]

CLARENCE

John, come here a minute.

JOHN

[*coming into the room*] What do you want?

CLARENCE

John, have you got any money you could lend me?

JOHN

With this week's allowance, I'll have about three dollars.

CLARENCE

That's no good. I've got to have enough to buy a new suit of clothes.

JOHN

Why don't you earn some money? That's what I'm going to do. I'm going to buy a bicycle — one of those new low kind, with both wheels the same size — you know, a safety.

CLARENCE

How are you going to earn that much money?

JOHN

I've got a job practically. Look, I found this ad in the paper. [*he hands* CLARENCE *a clipping from his pocket.*]

CLARENCE

[*reading*] "Wanted, an energetic young man to handle household necessity that sells on sight. Liberal commissions. Apply 312 West Fourteenth Street, Tuesday from eight to twelve." Listen, John, let me have that job.

JOHN

Why should I give you my job? They're hard to get.

CLARENCE

But I've got to have a new suit of clothes.

JOHN

Maybe I could get a job for both of us. [*the doorbell rings.*] I'll tell you what I'll do, I'll ask the man.

FATHER

[*hurrying to the foot of the stairs*] Vinnie! Cora! The cab's here. Hurry up! [*goes through the arch toward the front door.*]

CLARENCE

John, we've both got to get down there early Tuesday
— the first thing.

JOHN

Oh, no you don't — I'm going alone. But I'll put in a
good word with the boss about you.

FATHER

[*off*] They'll be right out. Vinnie! Cora! [*he comes
back to the foot of the stairs and calls up.*] Are you
coming? The cab's waiting!

VINNIE

[*from upstairs*] We heard you, Clare. We'll be down
in a minute.

[FATHER *comes into the room.*]

FATHER

John, go upstairs and hurry them down.

[JOHN *goes upstairs.* FATHER *crosses
to the window and looks out, then con-
sults his watch.*]

FATHER

What's the matter with those women? Don't they know
cabs cost money? Clarence, go see what's causing this
infernal delay!

[CLARENCE *goes out to the hall.*]

CLARENCE

Here they come, Father.

> [MARY *comes sedately downstairs. She passes* CLARENCE *without a glance and goes to* FATHER.]

MARY

Goodbye, Mr. Day. I can't tell you how much I appreciate your hospitality.

FATHER

Not at all! Not at all!

> [VINNIE *and* CORA *appear at top of stairs and come down.* JOHN *follows with the bags and takes them out.*]

CORA

Goodbye, Clarence. [*she starts into the room.*]

FATHER

Cora, we can say goodbye to you on the sidewalk.

VINNIE

There's no hurry. Their train doesn't go until one-thirty.

FATHER

Cabs cost money. If they have any waiting to do they ought to do it at the Grand Central Depot. They've got a waiting-room there just *for* that.

VINNIE

[*to* MARY] If there's one thing Mr. Day can't stand it's to keep a cab waiting.

CORA

It's been so nice seeing you again, Clarence. [*she kisses him.*]

> [MARGARET *enters with a box of lunch.*]

MARGARET

Here's the lunch.

FATHER

All right. All right. Give it to me. Let's get started.

> [MARGARET *gives it to him and exits.*]

CORA

Where's John?

FATHER

He's outside. Come on. [*leads the way.* CORA *and* VINNIE *follow.* MARY *starts.*]

CLARENCE

Mary, aren't you going even to shake hands with me?

MARY

I don't think I'd better. You may remember that when I get too close to you you feel contaminated. [*starts out.* CLARENCE *follows her.*]

CLARENCE

Mary! [*she stops in the arch. He goes to her.*] You're going to write me, aren't you?

MARY

Are you going to write first?

CLARENCE

[*resolutely*] No, Mary. There are times when a man has to be firm.

[JOHN *enters.*]

JOHN

Mary, Mother says you'd better hurry out before Father starts yelling. It's Sunday.

MARY

Goodbye, John. I'm very happy to have made *your* acquaintance.

[*She walks out. We hear the door close.* JOHN *goes out.* CLARENCE *takes a step toward the door, stops, suffers a moment, then turns to the writing desk, takes paper and pen and ink to the table, and sits down to write a letter.*]

CLARENCE

[*writing*] Dear Mary —

CURTAIN

SCENE II

The same.
Two days later. The breakfast table.
HARLAN *and* WHITNEY *are at the table, ready to start breakfast.* CLARENCE *is near the window reading the paper. The places of* JOHN *and* VINNIE *and* FATHER *are empty.* NORA, *a new maid, is serving the fruit and cereal.* NORA *is heavily built and along toward middle age. The doorbell rings and we hear the postman's whistle.* CLARENCE *drops the paper and looks out the window toward the door.* NORA *starts toward the arch.*

CLARENCE

Never mind, Nora. It's the postman. I'll go. [*he runs out through the arch.*]

WHITNEY

[*to* NORA] You forgot the sugar. It goes here between me and Father.

> [CLARENCE *comes back with three or four letters which he sorts eagerly. Then his face falls in utter dejection.* FATHER *comes down the stairs.*]

FATHER

Good morning, boys! John late? [*he shouts*] John! John! Hurry down to your breakfast.

CLARENCE

John had his breakfast early, Father, and went out to see about something.

FATHER

See about what?

CLARENCE

John and I thought we'd work this summer and earn some money.

FATHER

Good! Sit down boys. [*goes to his chair.*]

CLARENCE

We saw an ad in the paper and John went down to see about it.

FATHER

Why didn't you go, too?

CLARENCE

I was expecting an answer to a letter I wrote, but it didn't come. Here's the mail. [*he seems depressed.*]

FATHER

[*sitting*] What kind of work is this you're planning to do?

CLARENCE

Sort of salesman, the ad said.

FATHER

Um-hum. Well, work never hurt anybody. It's good for them. But if you're going to work, work hard. King Solomon had the right idea about work. "Whatever thy hand findeth to do," Solomon said, "do thy damnedest!" Where's your mother?

NORA

If you please, sir, Mrs. Day doesn't want any breakfast. She isn't feeling well, so she went back upstairs to lie down again.

FATHER

[*uneasily*] Now, why does your mother do that to me? She knows it just upsets my day when she doesn't come down to breakfast. Clarence, go tell your mother I'll be up to see her before I start for the office.

CLARENCE

Yes, sir. [*he goes upstairs.*]

HARLAN

What's the matter with Mother?

FATHER

There's nothing the matter with your mother. Perfectly healthy woman. She gets an ache or a twinge and instead of being firm about it, she just gives in to it.

[*The postman whistles. Then the door-bell rings.* NORA *answers it.*]

Boys, after breakfast you find out what your mother wants you to do today. Whitney, you take care of Harlan.

> [N O R A *comes back with a special-delivery letter.*]

N O R A

It's a special delivery.

> [*She hands it to* F A T H E R, *who tears it open at once.* C L A R E N C E *comes rushing down the stairs.*]

C L A R E N C E

Was that the postman again?

W H I T N E Y

It was a special delivery.

C L A R E N C E

Yes? Where is it?

W H I T N E Y

It was for Father.

C L A R E N C E

[*again disappointed*] Oh — [*he sits at the table.*]

> [F A T H E R *has opened the letter and is reading it. Bewildered, he turns it over and looks at the signature.*]

FATHER

I don't understand this at all. Here's a letter from some woman I never even heard of.

> [FATHER *tackles the letter again.* CLARENCE *sees the envelope, picks it up, looks at the postmark, worried.*]

CLARENCE

Father!

FATHER

Oh, God!

CLARENCE

What is it, Father?

FATHER

This is the damnedest nonsense I ever read! As far as I can make out this woman claims that she sat on my lap and I didn't like it.

> [CLARENCE *begins to turn red.* FATHER *goes on reading a little further and then holds the letter over in front of* CLARENCE.]

Can you make out what that word is?

> [CLARENCE *begins feverishly to read as much as possible, but* FATHER *cuts in.*]

No, that word right there. [*he points.*]

CLARENCE

It looks like — "curiosity."

> [FATHER *withdraws the letter,* CLAR-
> ENCE'S *eyes following it hungrily.*]

FATHER

[*reads*] "I only opened your letter as a matter of curiosity." [*breaks off reading aloud as he turns the page.*]

CLARENCE

Yes? Go on.

FATHER

Why, this gets worse and worse! It just turns into a lot
of sentimental lovey-dovey mush. [*crushes the letter,
stalks across the room, and throws it into the fireplace,*
CLARENCE *watching him with dismay.*] Is this
someone's idea of a practical joke? Why must I be
the butt —

> [VINNIE *comes hurrying down the
> stairs. Her hair is down in two braids
> over her shoulder. She is wearing a lacy
> combing jacket over her corset cover, and
> a striped petticoat.*]

VINNIE

What's the matter, Clare? What's wrong?

FATHER

[*going to her*] Nothing wrong — just a damn fool letter. How are you, Vinnie?

VINNIE

[*weakly*] I don't feel well. I thought you needed me, but if you don't I'll go back to bed.

FATHER

No, now that you're here, sit down with us. [*he moves out her chair.*] Get some food in your stomach. Do you good.

VINNIE

[*protesting*] I don't feel like eating anything, Clare.

> [NORA *enters with a tray of bacon and eggs, stops at the serving table.*]

FATHER

[*heartily*] That's all the more reason why you should eat. Build up your strength! [*he forces* VINNIE *into her chair and turns to speak to* NORA, *who has her back to him.*] Here— [*then to* CLARENCE] What's this one's name?

CLARENCE

Nora.

FATHER

Nora! Give Mrs. Day some of the bacon and eggs.

VINNIE

No, Clare!

> [NORA, *however, has gone to* VINNIE's *side with the platter.*]

No, take it away, Nora. I don't even want to smell it.

[*The maid retreats, and serves* FA-
THER ; *then* CLARENCE ; *then serves
coffee and exits.*]

FATHER

Vinnie, it's just weak to give in to an ailment. Any
disease can be cured by firmness. What you need is
strength of character.

VINNIE

I don't know why you object to my complaining a little.
I notice when you have a headache you yell and groan
and swear enough.

FATHER

Of course I yell! That's to prove to the headache that
I'm stronger than it is. I can usually swear it right out
of my system.

VINNIE

This isn't a headache. I think I've caught some kind
of a germ. There's a lot of sickness around. Several of
my friends have had to send for the doctor. I may have
the same thing.

FATHER

I'll bet this is all your imagination, Vinnie. You hear of
a lot of other people having some disease and then you
get scared and think you have it yourself. So you go to
bed and send for the doctor. The doctor — all poppy-
cock!

VINNIE

I didn't say anything about my sending for the doctor.

FATHER

I should hope not. Doctors think they know a damn lot, but they don't.

VINNIE

But Clare, dear, when people are seriously ill you have to do something.

FATHER

Certainly you have to do something! Cheer 'em up — that's the way to cure 'em!

VINNIE

[*with slight irony*] How would you go about cheering them up?

FATHER

I? I'd tell 'em — bah!

> [VINNIE, *out of exasperation and weakness, begins to cry.* FATHER *looks at her amazed.*]

What have I done now?

VINNIE

Oh, Clare — hush up! [*she moves from the table to the sofa, where she tries to control her crying.* HARLAN *slides out of his chair and runs over to her.*] Harlan dear, keep away from Mother. You might catch what she's got. Whitney, if you've finished your breakfast —

WHITNEY

[*rising*] Yes, Mother.

VINNIE

I promised Mrs. Whitehead to send over Margaret's recipe for floating-island pudding. Margaret has it all written out. And take Harlan with you.

WHITNEY

All right, Mother. I hope you feel better.

> [WHITNEY *and* HARLAN *exit.* FA-
> THER *goes over and sits beside* VINNIE
> *on the sofa.*]

FATHER

Vinnie. [*contritely*] I didn't mean to upset you. I was just trying to help. [*he pats her hand.*] When you take to your bed I have a damned lonely time around here. So when I see you getting it into your head that you're sick, I want to do something about it. [*he continues to pat her hand vigorously with what he thinks is reassurance.*] Just because some of your friends have given in to this is no reason why you should imagine you're sick, Vinnie.

VINNIE

[*snatching her hand away*] Oh, stop, Clare! — get out of this house and go to your office!

> [FATHER *is a little bewildered and
> somewhat indignant at this rebuff to his*

> *tenderness. He gets up and goes out into the hall, comes back with his hat and stick, and marches out of the house, slamming the door.* VINNIE *rises and starts toward the stairs.*]

CLARENCE

I'm sorry you're not feeling well, Mother.

VINNIE

Oh, I'll be all right, Clarence. Remember last fall I had a touch of this and I was all right the next morning.

CLARENCE

Are you sure you don't want the doctor?

VINNIE

Oh, no. I really don't need him — and besides doctors worry your father. I don't want him to be upset.

CLARENCE

Is there anything I can do for you?

VINNIE

Ask Margaret to send me up a cup of tea. I'll try to drink it. I'm going back to bed.

CLARENCE

Do you mind if John and I go out today or will you need us?

VINNIE

You run right along. I just want to be left alone.

[*She exits up the stairs.* CLARENCE
*starts for the fireplace eager to retrieve
Mary's letter.* NORA *enters. He stops.*]

CLARENCE

Oh!—Nora—will you take a cup of tea up to Mrs.
Day in her room?

NORA

Yes, sir. [*exits.*]

[CLARENCE *hurries around the table,
gets the crumpled letter, and starts to
read it feverishly. He reads quickly to
the end, then draws a deep, happy breath.
The door slams. He puts the letter in his
pocket.* JOHN *enters, carrying two
heavy packages.*]

CLARENCE

Did you get the job?

JOHN

Yes, for both of us. Look, I've got it with me.

CLARENCE

What is it?

JOHN

Medicine.

CLARENCE

[*dismayed*] Medicine! You took a job for us to go out
and sell medicine!

JOHN

But it's wonderful medicine. [*gets a bottle out of the package and reads from the label.*] "Bartlett's Beneficent Balm — A Boon to Mankind." Look what it cures! [*he hands the bottle to* CLARENCE.]

CLARENCE

[*reading*] "A sovereign cure for colds, coughs, catarrh, asthma, quinsy, and sore throat; poor digestion, summer complaint, colic, dyspepsia, heartburn, and shortness of breath; lumbago, rheumatism, heart disease, giddiness, and women's complaints; nervous prostration, St. Vitus' dance, jaundice, and la grippe; proud flesh, pink eye, seasickness, and pimples." [*As* CLARENCE *has read off the list he has become more and more impressed.*]

JOHN

See?

CLARENCE

Say, that sounds all right!

JOHN

It's made "from a secret formula known only to Dr. Bartlett."

CLARENCE

He must be quite a doctor!

JOHN

[*enthusiastically*] It sells for a dollar a bottle and we get twenty-five cents commission on every bottle.

CLARENCE

Well, where does he want us to sell it?

JOHN

He's given us the territory of all Manhattan Island.

CLARENCE

That's bully! Anybody that's sick at all ought to need a bottle of this. Let's start by calling on friends of Father and Mother.

JOHN

That's a good idea. But wait a minute. Suppose they ask us if we use it at our house?

CLARENCE

[*a little worried*] Oh, yes. It would be better if we could say we did.

JOHN

But we can't because we haven't had it here long enough.

> [NORA *enters with a tray with a cup of tea. She goes to the table and puts the sugar bowl and cream pitcher on it.*]

CLARENCE

Is that the tea for Mrs. Day?

NORA

Yes.

> [*The suspicion of a good idea dawns on* CLARENCE.]

CLARENCE

I'll take it up to her. You needn't bother.

NORA

Thank you. Take it up right away while it's hot. [*she exits.* CLARENCE *watches her out.*]

CLARENCE

[*eyeing* JOHN] Mother wasn't feeling well this morning.

JOHN

What was the matter with her?

CLARENCE

I don't know — she was just complaining.

JOHN

[*getting the idea immediately and consulting the bottle*] Well, it says here it's good for women's complaints.

[*They look at each other.* CLARENCE *opens the bottle and smells its contents.* JOHN *leans over and takes a sniff, too. Then he nods to* CLARENCE, *who quickly reaches for a spoon and measures out a teaspoonful, which he puts into the tea.* JOHN, *wanting to be sure* MOTHER *has enough to cure her, pours still more into the tea from the bottle as the curtain falls.*]

[THE CURTAIN *remains down for a few*

seconds to denote a lapse of three hours.]
[*When the curtain rises again, the breakfast things have been cleared and the
room is in order.* HARLAN *is kneeling
on* FATHER'S *chair looking out the window as if watching for someone.* MAR-
GARET *comes down from upstairs.*]

MARGARET

Has your father come yet?

HARLAN

Not yet.

[NORA *enters from downstairs with a
steaming tea-kettle and a towel and meets*
MARGARET *in the hall.*]

MARGARET

Hurry that upstairs. The doctor's waiting for it. I've
got to go out.

NORA

Where are you going?

MARGARET

I have to go and get the minister.

[NORA *goes upstairs.*]

HARLAN

There's a cab coming up the street.

MARGARET

Well, I hope it's him, poor man — but a cab doesn't sound like your father. [*she hurries downstairs.*]

[HARLAN *sees something through the window, then rushes to the stairwell and shouts down to* MARGARET.]

HARLAN

Yes, it's Father. Whitney got him all right. [*runs back to the window. The front door slams and* FATHER *crosses the arch and hurries upstairs.* WHITNEY *comes into the room.*] What took you so long?

WHITNEY

Long? I wasn't long. I went right down on the elevated and got Father right away and we came all the way back in a *cab*.

HARLAN

I thought you were never coming.

WHITNEY

Well, the horse didn't go very fast at first. The cabby whipped him and swore at him and still he wouldn't gallop. Then Father spoke to the horse personally — How is Mother?

HARLAN

I don't know. The doctor's up there now.

WHITNEY

Well, she'd better be good and sick or Father may be mad at me for getting him up here — 'specially in a cab.

[FATHER *comes down the stairs muttering to himself.*]

FATHER

[*indignantly*] Well, huh! — It seems to me I ought to be shown a little consideration. I guess I've got some feelings, too!

WHITNEY

[*hopefully*] Mother's awfully sick, isn't she?

FATHER

How do I know? I wasn't allowed to stay in the same room with her.

WHITNEY

Did the doctor put you out?

FATHER

No, it was your mother, damn it! [*he goes out and hangs up his hat and stick, then returns.* FATHER *may be annoyed, but he is also worried.*] You boys keep quiet around here today.

WHITNEY

She must be pretty sick.

FATHER

She must be, Whitney! I don't know! Nobody ever tells me anything in this house. Not a damn thing!

[DR. HUMPHREYS *comes down the stairs. He's the family-doctor type of the period, with just enough whiskers to make him impressive. He carries his satchel.*]

DR. HUMPHREYS

Mrs. Day is quieter now.

FATHER

How sick is she? What's the matter with her?

DR. HUMPHREYS

She's a pretty sick woman, Mr. Day. I had given her a sedative just before you came — and after you left the room I had to give her another. Have you a telephone?

FATHER

A telephone! No — I don't believe in them. Why?

DR. HUMPHREYS

Well, it would only have saved me a few steps. I'll be back in ten minutes. [*he turns to go.*]

FATHER

Wait a minute — I think I'm entitled to know what's the matter with my wife.

[DR. HUMPHREYS *turns back.*]

DR. HUMPHREYS

What did Mrs. Day have for breakfast this morning?

FATHER

She didn't eat anything — not a thing.

DR. HUMPHREYS

Are you sure?

FATHER

I tried to get her to eat something, but she wouldn't.

DR. HUMPHREYS

[*almost to himself*] I can't understand it.

FATHER

Understand what?

DR. HUMPHREYS

These violent attacks of nausea. It's almost as though she were poisoned.

FATHER

Poisoned!

DR. HUMPHREYS

I'll try not to be gone more than ten or fifteen minutes. [*he exits.*]

FATHER

[*trying to reassure himself*] Damn doctors! They never know what's the matter with anybody. Well, he'd better get your mother well, and damn soon or he'll hear from me.

WHITNEY

Mother's going to get well, isn't she?

[F A T H E R *looks at* W H I T N E Y *sharply*
as though he is a little angry at anyone
even raising the question.]

FATHER

Of course she's going to get well!

HARLAN

[*running to* F A T H E R] I hope she gets well soon. When
Mamma stays in bed it's lonesome.

FATHER

Yes, it is, Harlan. It's lonesome. [*he looks around the*
room and finds it pretty empty.] What were you boys
supposed to do today?

WHITNEY

I was to learn the rest of my catechism.

FATHER

Well, if that's what your mother wanted you to do,
you'd better do it.

WHITNEY

I know it — I think.

FATHER

You'd better be sure.

WHITNEY

I can't be sure unless somebody hears me. Will you hear
me?

FATHER

[*with sudden willingness to be useful*] All right. I'll
hear you, Whitney.

> [WHITNEY *goes to the mantel and gets*
> VINNIE'S *prayer book.* FATHER *sits
> on the sofa.* HARLAN *climbs up beside
> him.*]

HARLAN

If Mamma's still sick will you read to me tonight?

FATHER

Of course I'll read to you.

> [WHITNEY *opens the prayer book and
> hands it to* FATHER.]

WHITNEY

Here it is, Father. Just the end of it. Mother knows
I know the rest. Look, start here. [*he points.*]

FATHER

All right. [*reading*] "How many parts are there in a
Sacrament?"

WHITNEY

[*reciting*] "Two; the outward visible sign, and the inward spiritual grace."

> [FATHER *nods in approval.*]

FATHER

"What is the outward visible sign or form in Baptism?"

WHITNEY

"Water; wherein the person is baptized, in the name of the Father, and of the Son, and of the Holy Ghost." You haven't been baptized, Father, have you?

FATHER

[*ignoring it*] "What is the inward and spirtual grace?"

WHITNEY

If you don't have to be baptized, why do I have to be confirmed?

FATHER

[*ignoring this even more*] "What is the inward and spiritual grace?"

WHITNEY

"A death unto sin, and a new birth unto righteousness; for being by nature born in sin, and the children of wrath, we are hereby made the children of grace." Is that why you get mad so much, Father — because you're a child of wrath?

FATHER

Whitney, mind your manners! You're not supposed to ask questions of your elders! "What is required of persons to be baptized?"

WHITNEY

"Repentance, whereby — whereby — " [*he pauses.*]

FATHER

[*quickly shutting the book and handing it to* WHITNEY] You don't know it well enough, Whitney. You'd better study it some more.

WHITNEY

Now?

FATHER

[*softening*] No, you don't have to do it now. Let's see, now, what can we do?

WHITNEY

Well, I was working with my tool chest out in the back yard. [*edges toward the arch.*]

FATHER

Better not do any hammering with your mother sick upstairs. You'd better stay here.

WHITNEY

I wasn't hammering — I was doing wood-carving.

FATHER

Well, Harlan — how about you? Shall we play some tiddle-dy-winks?

HARLAN

[*edging toward* WHITNEY] I was helping Whitney.

FATHER

Oh — all right. [*the boys go out.* FATHER *goes to the stairwell.*] Boys, don't do any shouting. We all have to be very quiet around here. [*he stands in the hall and looks up toward* VINNIE, *worried. Then he tiptoes across the room and stares gloomily out of the window. Then he tiptoes back into the hall and goes to the rail of the basement stairs, and calls quietly.*] Margaret! [*there is no answer and he raises his voice a little.*] Margaret! [*there is still no answer and he lets loose.*] Margaret! Why don't you answer when you hear me calling?

> [*At this moment* MARGARET, *hat on, appears in the arch from the right, having come through the front door.*]

MARGARET

Sh — sh —

> [FATHER *turns quickly and sees* MARGARET.]

FATHER

Oh, there you are!

MARGARET

[*reprovingly*] We must all be quiet, Mr. Day — Mrs. Day is very sick.

FATHER

[*testily*] I know she's sick. That's what I wanted you for. You go up and wait outside her door in case she needs anything.

> [MARGARET *starts upstairs.*]

And what were you doing out of the house, anyway?

MARGARET

I was sent for the minister.

FATHER

[*startled*] The minister!

MARGARET

Yes, he'll be right in. He's paying off the cab.

> [MARGARET *continues upstairs. The door slams.* THE REVEREND DR. LLOYD *appears in the archway and meets* FATHER *in the hall.*]

DR. LLOYD

I was deeply shocked to hear of Mrs. Day's illness. I hope I can be of some service. Will you take me up to her?

FATHER

[*with a trace of hostility*] She's resting now. She can't be disturbed.

DR. LLOYD

But I've been summoned.

FATHER

The doctor will be back in a few minutes and we'll see what he has to say about it. You'd better come in and wait.

DR. LLOYD

Thank you. [*comes into the room.* FATHER *follows him reluctantly.*] Mrs. Day has been a tower of strength in the parish. Everyone liked her so much. Yes, she was a fine woman.

FATHER

I wish to God you wouldn't talk about Mrs. Day as if she were dead.

> [NORA *comes down the stairs and looks into the room.*]

NORA

Is the doctor back yet?

FATHER

No. Does she need him?

NORA

She's kinda' restless. She's talking in her sleep and twisting and turning. [*she goes downstairs.* FATHER *looks up toward* VINNIE'S *room, worried, then looks angrily toward the front door.*]

FATHER

That doctor said he'd be right back. [*he goes to the window.*]

MARGARET

[*coming downstairs*] Here comes the doctor. I was watching for him out the window. [*she goes to the front door. A moment later* DR. HUMPHREYS *enters.*]

FATHER

Well, doctor — seems to me that was a pretty long ten minutes.

DR. HUMPHREYS

[*indignantly*] See here, Mr. Day, if I'm to be respon-
sible for Mrs. Day's health, I must be allowed to handle
this case in my own way.

FATHER

Well, you can't handle it if you're out of the house.

DR. HUMPHREYS

[*flaring*] I left this house because —

> [DR. SOMERS, *an imposing medical fig-
> ure, enters and stops at* DR. HUM-
> PHREYS'S *side.*]

This is Dr. Somers.

DR. SOMERS

How do you do?

DR. HUMPHREYS

I felt that Mrs. Day's condition warranted my getting
Dr. Somers here as soon as possible for consultation. I
hope that meets with your approval.

FATHER

[*a little awed*] Why, yes, of course. Anything that can
be done.

DR. HUMPHREYS

Upstairs, doctor! [*the two doctors go upstairs.* FA-
THER *turns back into the room, obviously shaken.*]

DR. LLOYD

Mrs. Day is in good hands now, Mr. Day. There's nothing you and I can do at the moment to help.

> [*After a moment's consideration* FA-THER *decides there is something that can be done to help. He goes to* DR. LLOYD. FATHER *indicates the seat in front of the table to* DR. LLOYD *and they both sit.*]

FATHER

Dr. Lloyd, there's something that's troubling Mrs. Day's mind. I think you know what I refer to.

DR. LLOYD

Yes — you mean the fact that you've never been baptized.

FATHER

I gathered you knew about it from your sermon last Sunday. [*looks at him a second with indignant memory.*] But let's not get angry. I think something had better be done about it.

DR. LLOYD

Yes, Mr. Day.

FATHER

When the doctors get through up there I want you to talk to Mrs. Day. I want you to tell her something.

DR. LLOYD

[*eagerly*] Yes, I'll be glad to.

FATHER

You're just the man to do it! She shouldn't be upset
about this — I want you to tell her that my being baptized would just be a lot of damn nonsense.

> [*This isn't what* DR. LLOYD *has ex-
> pected and it is hardly his idea of how to
> help* MRS. DAY.]

DR. LLOYD

But, Mr. Day!

FATHER

No, she'd take your word on a thing like that — and
we've got to do everything we can to help her now.

DR. LLOYD

[*rising*] But baptism is one of the sacraments of the
Church —

FATHER

[*rising*] You're her minister and you're supposed to
bring her comfort and peace of mind.

DR. LLOYD

But the solution is so simple. It would take only your
consent to be baptized.

FATHER

That's out of the question! And I'm surprised that a grown man like you should suggest such a thing.

DR. LLOYD

If you're really concerned about Mrs. Day's peace of mind, don't you think —

FATHER

Now see here — if you're just going to keep her stirred up about this, I'm not going to let you see her at all. [*he turns away.* DR. LLOYD *follows him.*]

DR. LLOYD

Now, Mr. Day, as you said, we must do everything we can — [*the doctors come downstairs.* FATHER *sees them.*]

FATHER

Well, doctor, how is she? What have you decided?

DR. HUMPHREYS

We've just left Mrs. Day. Is there a room we could use for our consultation?

FATHER

Of course.

[MARGARET *starts downstairs.*]

Margaret, you go back upstairs! I don't want Mrs. Day left alone!

MARGARET

I have to do something for the doctor. I'll go back up as soon as I get it started.

FATHER

Well, hurry. And, Margaret, show these gentlemen downstairs to the billiard room.

MARGARET

Yes, sir. This way, doctor — downstairs. [*exits, followed by* DR. SOMERS. FATHER *delays* DR. HUMPHREYS.]

FATHER

Dr. Humphreys, you know now, don't you — this isn't serious, is it?

DR. HUMPHREYS

After we've had our consultation we'll talk to you, Mr. Day.

FATHER

But surely you must —

DR. HUMPHREYS

Just rest assured that Dr. Somers will do everything that is humanly possible.

FATHER

Why, you don't mean —

DR. HUMPHREYS

We'll try not to be long. [*exits.* FATHER *turns and looks at* DR. LLOYD. *He is obviously frightened.*]

FATHER

This Dr. Somers — I've heard his name often — he's very well thought of, isn't he?

DR. LLOYD

Oh, yes indeed.

FATHER

If Vinnie's really — if anyone could help her, he could — don't you think?

DR. LLOYD

A very fine physician. But there's a greater Help, ever present in the hour of need. Let us turn to Him in prayer. Let us kneel and pray.

> [FATHER *looks at him, straightens, then walks to the other side of the room.*]

Let us kneel and pray.

> [FATHER *finally bows his head.* DR. LLOYD *looks at him and, not kneeling himself, raises his head and speaks simply in prayer.*]

Oh, Lord, look down from Heaven — behold, visit, and relieve this Thy servant who is grieved with sickness, and extend to her Thy accustomed goodness. We know she has sinned against Thee in thought, word, and deed. Have mercy on her, O Lord, have mercy on this miserable sinner. Forgive her —

FATHER

She's not a miserable sinner and you know it! [*then* FATHER *speaks directly to the Deity.*] O God! You know Vinnie's not a miserable sinner. She's a damn fine woman! She shouldn't be made to suffer. It's got to stop, I tell You, it's got to stop!

> [VINNIE *appears on the stairway in her nightgown.*]

VINNIE

What's the matter, Clare? What's wrong?

FATHER

[*not hearing her*] Have mercy, I say, have mercy, damn it!

VINNIE

What's the matter, Clare? What's wrong?

> [FATHER *turns, sees* VINNIE, *and rushes to her.*]

FATHER

Vinnie, what are you doing down here? You shouldn't be out of bed. You get right back upstairs. [*he now has his arms around her.*]

VINNIE

Oh, Clare, I heard you call. Do you need me?

FATHER

[*deeply moved*] Vinnie — I know now how much I need you. Get well, Vinnie. I'll be baptized. I promise. I'll be baptized.

VINNIE

You will? Oh, Clare!

FATHER

I'll do anything. We'll go to Europe, just we two — you won't have to worry about the children or the household accounts —

> [VINNIE *faints against* FATHER'S *shoulder.*]

Vinnie! [*he stoops to lift her.*]

DR. LLOYD

I'll get the doctor. But don't worry, Mr. Day — she'll be all right now.

> [FATHER *lifts* VINNIE *up in his arms.*]

Bless you for what you've done, Mr. Day.

FATHER

What did I do?

DR. LLOYD

You promised to be baptized!

FATHER

[*aghast*] I did? [*with horror* FATHER *realizes he has been betrayed — and by himself.*] *OH, GOD!*

CURTAIN

A C T   I I I

SCENE I

The same.
A month later. Mid-afternoon.
VINNIE *is seated on the sofa embroidering petit point.*
MARGARET *enters, as usual uncomfortable at being*
upstairs.

MARGARET

You wanted to speak to me, ma'am?

VINNIE

Yes, Margaret, about tomorrow morning's breakfast —
we must plan it very carefully.

MARGARET

[*puzzled*] Mr. Day hasn't complained to me about his
breakfasts lately. As a matter of fact, I've been blessing
my luck!

VINNIE

Oh, no, it's not that. But tomorrow morning I'd like something for his breakfast that would surprise him.

MARGARET

[*doubtfully*] Surprising Mr. Day is always a bit of a risk, ma'am. My motto with him has always been "Let well enough alone."

VINNIE

But if we think of something he especially likes, Margaret — what would you say to kippers?

MARGARET

Well, I've served him kippers, but I don't recall his ever saying he liked them.

VINNIE

He's never said he didn't like them, has he?

MARGARET

They've never got a stamp on the floor out of him one way or the other.

VINNIE

If Mr. Day doesn't say he doesn't like a thing you can assume that he does. Let's take a chance on kippers, Margaret.

MARGARET

Very well, ma'am. [*she starts out.*]

ACT III SCENE I

VINNIE

". . . Surprising Mr. Day is always a bit of a risk ma'am. . . ."

VINNIE

[*innocently*] And, Margaret, you'd better have enough breakfast for two extra places.

MARGARET

[*knowingly*] Oh — so that's it! We're going to have company again.

VINNIE

Yes, my cousin, Miss Cartwright, and her friend are coming back from Springfield. I'm afraid they'll get here just about breakfast time.

MARGARET

Well, in that case I'd better make some of my Sunday morning hot biscuits, too.

VINNIE

Yes. We *know* Mr. Day likes those.

MARGARET

I've been getting him to church with them for the last fifteen years. [*the door slams.* MARGARET *goes to the arch and looks.*] Oh, it's Mr. Clarence, ma'am. [*goes off downstairs and* CLARENCE *enters with a large package.*]

CLARENCE

Here it is, Mother. [*he puts it on the table.*]

VINNIE

Oh, it was still in the store! They hadn't sold it! I'm so thrilled. Didn't you admire it, Clarence? [she hurries over to the table.]

CLARENCE

Well, it's unusual.

VINNIE

[unwrapping the package] You know, I saw this down there the day before I got sick. I was walking through the bric-a-brac section and it caught my eye. I was so tempted to buy it! And all the time I lay ill I just couldn't get it out of my head. I can't understand how it could stay in the store all this time without somebody snatching it up. [she takes it out of the box. It is a large china pug dog.] Isn't that the darlingest thing you ever saw! It does need a ribbon, though. I've got the very thing somewhere. Oh, yes, I know. [goes to the side table and gets a red ribbon out of the drawer.]

CLARENCE

Isn't John home yet?

VINNIE

I haven't seen him. Why?

CLARENCE

Well, you know we've been working, and John went down to collect our money.

VINNIE

That's fine. [*she ties the ribbon around the dog's neck.*]
Oh, Clarence, I have a secret for just the two of us; who
do you think is coming to visit us tomorrow? — Cousin
Cora and Mary.

CLARENCE

Yes, I know.

VINNIE

How did you know?

CLARENCE

I happened to get a letter.

[JOHN *enters, carrying two packages
of medicine.*]

VINNIE

John, did you ever see anything so sweet?

JOHN

What is it?

VINNIE

It's a pug dog. Your father would never let me have a
real one, but he can't object to one made of china. This
ribbon needs pressing. I'll take it down and have Margaret do it right away. [*exits with the beribboned pug
dog.*]

CLARENCE

What did you bring home more medicine for? [*then,
with sudden fright*] Dr. Bartlett paid us off, didn't he?

JOHN

Oh, yes!

CLARENCE

[*heaving a great sigh of relief*] You had me scared for a minute. When I went down to McCreery's to get that pug dog for Mother, I ordered the daisiest suit you ever saw. Dr. Bartlett owed us sixteen dollars apiece, and the suit was only fifteen. Wasn't that lucky? Come on, give me my money.

JOHN

Clarence, Dr. Bartlett paid us off in medicine.

CLARENCE

You let him pay us off with that old Benificent Balm!

JOHN

Well, he thanked us, too, for our services to mankind.

CLARENCE

[*in agony*] But my suit!

JOHN

You'll just have to wait for your suit.

CLARENCE

I can't wait! I've got to have it tomorrow — and besides they're making the alterations. I've got to pay for it this afternoon! Fifteen dollars!

JOHN

[*helpfully*] Why don't you offer them fifteen bottles of medicine?

[CLARENCE *gives it a little desperate thought.*]

CLARENCE

They wouldn't take it. McCreery's don't sell medicine.

[JOHN *is by the window and looks out.*]

JOHN

That's too bad. Here comes Father.

CLARENCE

I'll have to brace him for that fifteen dollars. I hate to do it, but I've got to — that's all — I've got to.

JOHN

I'm not going to be here when you do. I'd better hide this somewhere, anyway. [*takes the packages and hurries upstairs. The door slams.* FATHER *enters and looks into the room.*]

CLARENCE

Good afternoon, sir.

FATHER

How's your mother, Clarence? Where is she?

CLARENCE

She's all right. She's downstairs with Margaret. Oh, Father —

[FATHER *goes off down the hall and we hear him calling downstairs.*]

FATHER

Vinnie! Vinnie! I'm home. [*comes back into the room, carrying his newspaper.*]

CLARENCE

Father, Mother will be well enough to go to church with us next Sunday.

FATHER

That's fine, Clarence. That's fine.

CLARENCE

Father, have you noticed that I haven't been kneeling down in church lately?

FATHER

Clarence, don't let your mother catch you at it.

CLARENCE

Then I've got to have a new suit of clothes right away!

FATHER

[*after a puzzled look*] Clarence, you're not even making sense!

CLARENCE

But a fellow doesn't feel right in cut-down clothes — especially your clothes. That's why I can't kneel down in church — I can't do anything in them you wouldn't do.

FATHER

Well, that's a damn good thing! If my old clothes make you behave yourself I don't think you ought to wear anything else.

CLARENCE

[*desperately*] *Oh, no!* You're you and I'm me! I want to be myself! Besides, you're older and there are things I've got to do that I wouldn't do at your age.

FATHER

Clarence, you should never do anything I wouldn't do.

CLARENCE

Oh, yes, — look, for instance: Suppose I should want to kneel down in front of a girl?

FATHER

Why in Heaven's name should you want to do a thing like that?

CLARENCE

Well, I've got to get married *sometime*. I've got to pro-pose to a girl *sometime*.

FATHER

[*exasperated*] Before you're married, you'll be earning your own clothes, I hope. Don't get the idea into your head I'm going to support you and a wife, too. Besides, at your age, Clarence —

CLARENCE

[*hastily*] Oh, I'm not going to be married right away, but for fifteen dollars I can get a good suit of clothes.

FATHER

[*bewildered and irritated*] Clarence! [*he stares at him.*]

     [*At this second,* VINNIE *comes through the arch.*]

Why, you're beginning to talk as crazy as your mother. [*he sees her.*] Oh, hello, Vinnie. How're you feeling today?

VINNIE

I'm fine, Clare. [*they kiss.*] You don't have to hurry home from the office every day like this.

     [CLARENCE *throws himself in the chair by the window, sick with disappointment.*]

FATHER

Business the way it is, no use going to the office at all.

VINNIE

But you haven't been to your club for weeks.

FATHER

Can't stand the damn place. You do look better, Vinnie. What did you do today? [*drops on the sofa.* VINNIE *stands behind the sofa. Her chatter does not succeed in diverting* FATHER *from his newspaper.*]

VINNIE

I took a long walk and dropped in to call on old Mrs. Whitehead.

FATHER

Well, that's fine.

VINNIE

And, Clare, it was the most fortunate thing that ever happened. I've got wonderful news for you! Who do you think was there? Mr. Morley!

FATHER

[*not placing him*] Morley?

VINNIE

You remember — that nice young minister who substituted for Dr. Lloyd one Sunday?

FATHER

Oh, yes! Bright young fellow, preached a good sensible sermon.

VINNIE

It was the only time I ever saw you put five dollars in the plate!

FATHER

Ought to be more ministers like him. I could get along with that young man without any trouble at all.

VINNIE

Well, Clare, his parish is in Audubon — you know, 'way up above Harlem.

FATHER

Is that so?

VINNIE

Isn't that wonderful? Nobody knows you up there. You'll be perfectly safe!

FATHER

Safe? Vinnie, what the devil are you talking about?

VINNIE

I've been all over everything with Mr. Morley and he's agreed to baptize you.

FATHER

Oh, he has — the young whippersnapper! Damn nice of him!

VINNIE

We can go up there any morning, Clare — we don't even have to make an appointment.

FATHER

Vinnie, you're just making a lot of plans for nothing. Who said I was going to be baptized at all?

VINNIE

[*aghast*] Why, Clare! *You* did!

FATHER

Now, Vinnie! —

VINNIE

You gave me your promise — your Sacred Promise.
You stood right on that spot and said: " I'll be baptized.
I promise — I'll be baptized."

FATHER

What if I did?

VINNIE

[*amazed, she comes down and faces him.*] Aren't you
a man of your word?

FATHER

[*rising*] Vinnie, that was under entirely different cir-
cumstances. We all thought you were dying, so natu-
rally I said that to make you feel better. As a matter
of fact, the doctor told me that's what cured you. So it
seems to me pretty ungrateful of you to press this matter
any further.

VINNIE

Clarence Day, you gave me your Sacred Promise!

FATHER

[*getting annoyed*] Vinnie, you were sick when I said
that. Now you're well again.

[MARGARET *enters with the pug dog,
which now has the freshly pressed ribbon
tied around its neck. She puts it on the
table.*]

MARGARET

Is that all right, Mrs. Day?

VINNIE

[*dismissingly*] That's fine, Margaret, thank you.

[MARGARET *exits*.]

My being well has nothing to do with it. You gave me your word! You gave the Lord your word. If you had seen how eager Mr. Morley was to bring you into the fold.

[FATHER, *trying to escape, has been moving toward the arch when suddenly the pug dog catches his eye and he stares at it fascinated*.]

And you're going to march yourself up to his church some morning before you go to the office and be christened. If you think for one minute that I'm going to —

FATHER

What in the name of Heaven is that?

VINNIE

If you think I'm going to let you add the sin of breaking your Solemn and Sacred Promise —

FATHER

I demand to know what that repulsive object is!

VINNIE

[*exasperated in her turn*] It's perfectly plain what it is — it's a pug dog!

FATHER

What's it doing in this house?

VINNIE

[*defiantly*] I wanted it and I bought it.

FATHER

You spent good money for that?

VINNIE

Clare, we're not talking about that! We're talking about you. Don't try to change the subject!

FATHER

How much did you pay for that atrocity?

VINNIE

I don't know. I sent Clarence down for it. Listen to me, Clare —

FATHER

Clarence, what did you pay for that?

CLARENCE

I didn't pay anything. I charged it.

FATHER

[*looking at* VINNIE] Charged it! I might have known. [*to* CLARENCE] How much was it?

CLARENCE

Fifteen dollars.

FATHER

Fifteen dollars for that eyesore?

VINNIE

[*to the rescue of the pug dog*] Don't you call that lovely work of art an eyesore! That will look beautiful sitting on a red cushion by the fireplace in the parlor.

FATHER

If that sits in the parlor, I won't! Furthermore, I don't even want it in the same house with me. Get it out of here! [*he starts for the stairs.*]

VINNIE

You're just using that for an excuse. You're not going to get out of this room until you set a date for your baptism.

> [**FATHER** *turns at the foot of the stairs.*]

FATHER

I'll tell you one thing! I'll never be baptized while that hideous monstrosity is in this house. [*he stalks upstairs.*]

VINNIE

[*calling after him*] All right! [*she goes to the pug dog.*] All right! It goes back this afternoon and he's christened first thing in the morning.

CLARENCE

But, Mother—

VINNIE

" Don't you call that lovely work of art an eyesore ! "

VINNIE

Clarence, you heard him say that he'd be baptized as soon as I got this pug dog out of the house. You hurry right back to McCreery's with it — and be sure they credit us with fifteen dollars.

[*The fifteen dollars rings a bell in* CLARENCE'S *mind.*]

CLARENCE

Oh, say, Mother, while I was at McCreery's, I happened to see a suit I would like very much and the suit was only fifteen dollars.

VINNIE

[*regretfully*] Well, Clarence, I think your suit will have to wait until after I get your father christened.

CLARENCE

[*hopefully*] No. I meant that since the suit cost just the same as the pug dog, if I exchanged the pug dog for the suit —

VINNIE

Why, yes! Then your suit wouldn't cost Father anything! Why, how bright of you, Clarence, to think of that!

CLARENCE

[*quickly*] I'd better start right away before McCreery's closes. [*they have collected the box, wrapper, and tissue paper.*]

VINNIE

Yes. Let's see. If we're going to take your father all
the way up to Audubon — Clarence, you stop at Ryerson & Brown's on your way back and tell them to have
a cab here at eight o'clock tomorrow morning.

CLARENCE

Mother, a cab! Do you think you ought to do that?

VINNIE

Well, we can't walk to Audubon.

CLARENCE

[*warningly*] But you know what a cab does to Father!

VINNIE

This is an important occasion.

CLARENCE

[*with a shrug*] All right! A brougham or a Victoria?

VINNIE

Get one of their best cabs — the kind they use at funer-
als.

CLARENCE

Those cost two dollars an hour! And if Father gets
mad —

VINNIE

Well, if your father starts to argue in the morning, you
remember —

CLARENCE

[*remembering his suit*] Oh, he agreed to it! We both heard him!

> [VINNIE *has removed the ribbon and is about to put the pug dog back in the box.*]

VINNIE

[*regretfully*] I did have my heart set on this. [*an idea comes to her.*] Still — if they didn't sell him in all that time, he might be safe there for a few more weeks. [*she gives the dog a reassuring pat and puts him in the box.*]

> [*She begins to sing "Sweet Marie" happily.* FATHER *comes down the stairs.* CLARENCE *takes his hat and the box and goes happily and quickly out.* FATHER *watches him.*]

I hope you notice that Clarence is returning the pug dog.

FATHER

That's a sign you're getting your faculties back.

> [VINNIE *is singing quietly to herself in a satisfied way.*]

Good to hear you singing again, Vinnie. [*suddenly remembering something*] Oh! — on my way uptown I stopped in at Tiffany's and bought you a little something. Thought you might like it. [*he takes out of his pocket a small ring-box and holds it out to her. She takes it.*]

VINNIE

Oh, Clare. [*she opens it eagerly.*] What a beautiful ring! [*she takes the ring out, puts it on her finger, and admires it.*]

FATHER

Glad if it pleases you. [*he settles down to his newspaper on the sofa.*]

VINNIE

I don't know how to thank you. [*she kisses him.*]

FATHER

It's thanks enough for me to have you up and around again. When you're sick, Vinnie, this house is like a tomb. There's no excitement.

VINNIE

[*sitting beside him*] Clare, this is the loveliest ring you ever bought me. Now that I have this, you needn't buy me any more rings.

FATHER

Well, if you don't want any more.

VINNIE

What I'd really like now is a nice diamond necklace.

FATHER

[*alarmed*] Vinnie, do you know how much a diamond necklace costs?

VINNIE

I know, Clare, but don't you see? — your giving me this
ring shows that I mean a little something to you. Now,
a diamond necklace —

FATHER

Good God, if you don't know by this time how I feel
about you! We've been married for twenty years and
I've loved you every minute of it.

VINNIE

What did you say? [*her eyes well with tears at* FA-
THER's *definite statement of his love.*]

FATHER

I said we'd been married twenty years and I've loved you
every minute of it. But if I have to buy out jewelry
stores to prove it — if I haven't shown it to you in my
words and actions, I might as well — [*he turns and sees*
VINNIE *dabbing her eyes and speaks with resignation.*]
What have I done now?

VINNIE

It's all right, Clare — I'm just so happy.

FATHER

Happy!

VINNIE

You said you loved me! And this beautiful ring —
that's something else I didn't expect. Oh, Clare, I love
surprises. [*she nestles against him.*]

FATHER

That's another thing I can't understand about you, Vinnie. Now, *I* like to know what to expect. Then I'm prepared to meet it.

VINNIE

[*putting her head on his shoulder*] Yes, I know. But, Clare, life would be pretty dull if we always knew what was coming.

FATHER

Well, it's certainly not dull around here. In this house you never know what's going to hit you tomorrow.

VINNIE

[*to herself*] Tomorrow! [*she starts to sing,* FATHER *listening to her happily.*]
    "Every daisy in the dell,
       Knows my secret, knows it well,
       And yet I dare not tell,
       Sweet Marie!"

CURTAIN

SCENE II

The same.
The next morning. Breakfast. All the family except JOHN *and* VINNIE *are at the table and in good spirits.*

ACT III SCENE I

FATHER

"Well it's certainly not dull around here. In this house you never know what is going to hit you to-morrow."

JOHN

[*entering*] Mother says she'll be right down. [*he sits at the table.*]

> [MAGGIE, *the new maid, enters with a plate of hot biscuits and serves* FATHER. *As* FATHER *takes a biscuit, he glances up at her and shows some little surprise.*]

FATHER

Who are you? What's your name?

MAGGIE

Margaret, sir.

FATHER

Can't be Margaret. We've got one Margaret in the house.

MAGGIE

At home they call me Maggie, sir.

FATHER

[*genially*] All right, Maggie.

> [MAGGIE *continues serving the biscuits.*]

Boys, if her name's Margaret, that's a good sign. Maybe she'll stay awhile. You know, boys, your mother used to be just the same about cooks as she is about maids. Never could keep them for some reason. Well, one day about fifteen years ago — yes, it was right after you were born, John — my, you were a homely baby.

[*They all laugh at* J O H N's *expense.*]

I came home that night all tired out and what did I find?
— no dinner, because the cook had left. Well, I decided
I'd had just about enough of that, so I just marched
over to the employment agency on Sixth Avenue and
said to the woman in charge: "Where do you keep the
cooks?" She tried to hold me up with a lot of red-tape
folderol, but I just walked into the room where the girls
were waiting, looked 'em over, saw Margaret, pointed at
her, and said: "I'll take that one." I walked her home,
she cooked dinner that night, and she's been cooking for
us ever since. Damn good cook, too. [*he stamps on the
floor three times.*]

> [V I N N I E *comes down the stairs dressed
> in white. Somehow she almost has the
> appearance of a bride going to her wed-
> ding.*]

VINNIE

Good morning, Clare. Good morning, boys.

> [*The boys and* F A T H E R *rise.* V I N N I E
> *takes her bonnet and gloves and lays
> them on the chair below the fireplace.*
> F A T H E R *goes to* V I N N I E's *chair and
> holds it out for her, glancing at her holi-
> day appearance.* V I N N I E *sits.*]

FATHER

Sit down, boys. [*as* FATHER *returns to his own chair, he notices that all of the boys are dressed in their Sunday best.*] Everyone's dressed up this morning. What's on the program for this fine day?

> [VINNIE, *who always postpones crises in the hope some miracle will aid her, postpones this one.*]

VINNIE

Well, this afternoon May Lewis's mother is giving a party for everyone in May's dancing class. Harlan's going to that.

HARLAN

I don't want to go, Mamma.

VINNIE

Why, Harlan, don't you want to go to a party and get ice cream and cake?

HARLAN

May Lewis always tries to kiss me.

> [*This is greeted with family laughter.*]

FATHER

[*genially*] When you get a little older, you won't object to girls' wanting to kiss you, will he, Clarence?

> [MARGARET *comes hurrying in.*]

MARGARET

What's wanting?

FATHER

Margaret, these kippers are *good*.

> [MARGARET *makes her usual deprecatory gesture toward him.*]

Haven't had kippers for a long time. I'm glad you remembered I like them.

MARGARET

Yes, sir.

> [MARGARET *and* VINNIE *exchange knowing looks.* MARGARET *goes out happy.*]

FATHER

What's got into Margaret this morning? Hot biscuits, too!

VINNIE

She knows you're fond of them.

> [*The doorbell rings.* MAGGIE *goes to answer it.* VINNIE *stirs nervously in her chair.*]

Who can that be? It can't be the mail man because he's been here.

FATHER

[*with sly humor*] Clarence has been getting a good

many special deliveries lately. Is that business deal going through, Clarence?

> [*The family has a laugh at* C L A R E N C E.
> M A G G I E *comes back into the arch with
> a suit box.*]

M A G G I E
This is for you, Mr. Day. Where shall I put it?

C L A R E N C E
[*hastily*] Oh, that's for me, I think. Take it upstairs,
Maggie.

F A T H E R
Wait a minute, Maggie, bring it here. Let's see it.

> [C L A R E N C E *takes the box from* M A G-
> G I E, *who exits. He holds it toward his
> father.*]

C L A R E N C E
See, it's for me, Father — Clarence Day, Jr.

F A T H E R
Let me look. Why, that's from McCreery's and it's
marked "Charge." What is it?

V I N N I E
It's all right, Clare. It's nothing for you to worry about.

F A T H E R
Well, at least I think I should know what's being
charged to me. What is it?

VINNIE

Now, Clare, stop your fussing. It's a new suit of clothes for Clarence and it's not costing you a penny.

FATHER

It's marked "Charge fifteen dollars" — it's costing me fifteen dollars. And I told Clarence —

VINNIE

Clare, can't you take my word it isn't costing you a penny?

FATHER

I'd like to have you explain why it isn't.

VINNIE

[*triumphantly*] Because Clarence took the pug dog back and got the suit instead.

FATHER

Of course, and they'll charge me fifteen dollars for the suit.

VINNIE

Nonsense, Clare. We gave them the pug dog for the suit. Don't you see?

FATHER

Then they'll charge me fifteen dollars for the pug dog.

VINNIE

But, Clare, they can't! We haven't got the pug dog. We sent that back.

FATHER

[*bewildered, but not convinced*] Now wait a minute, Vinnie. There's something wrong with your reasoning.

VINNIE

I'm surprised, Clare, and you're supposed to be so good at figures. Why, it's perfectly clear to me.

FATHER

Vinnie! They're going to charge me for one thing or the other.

VINNIE

Don't you let them!

[FATHER *gets up and throws his napkin on the table.*]

FATHER

Well, McCreery's aren't giving away suits and they aren't giving away pug dogs. [*he walks over to the window in his irritation.*] Can't you get it through your — [*looking out the window*] Oh, God!

VINNIE

What is it, Clare? What's wrong?

FATHER

Don't anybody answer the door.

VINNIE

Who is it? Who's coming?

FATHER

Those damn women are back!

WHITNEY

What women?

FATHER

Cora and that little idiot.

> [CLARENCE *dashes madly up the stairs clutching the box containing his new suit.*]

They're moving in on us again, bag and baggage!

> [*The doorbell rings.*]

Don't let them in!

VINNIE

Clarence Day, as if we could turn our own relatives away!

FATHER

Tell them to get back in that cab and drive right on to Ohio. If they're extravagant enough to take cabs when horse cars run right by our door —

> [MAGGIE *crosses the hall to answer the doorbell.*]

VINNIE

Now, Clare — you be quiet and behave yourself. They're here and there's nothing you can do about it. [*she starts toward the hall.*]

FATHER

[*shouting after her*] Well, why do they always pounce on us without warning? — the damn gypsies!

VINNIE

[*from the arch*] Shhh! — Clare! [*then in her best welcoming tone*] Cora! Mary! It's so nice to have you back again.

CORA

How are you, Vinnie? We've been so worried about you.

VINNIE

Oh, I'm fine now!

> [CORA *and* MARY *and* VINNIE *enter and* CORA *sweeps right down into the room.*]

CORA

Hello, Harlan! Whitney! Well, Cousin Clare. Here we are again! [*kisses* FATHER *on the cheek. He draws back sternly.* MARY *looks quickly around the room for* CLARENCE, *then greets and is greeted by the other boys.*] And John! Where's Clarence?

MARY

Yes, where is Clarence?

VINNIE

John, go find Clarence and tell him that Cora and Mary are here.

JOHN

Yes, Mother. [*goes upstairs.*]

VINNIE

You got here just in time to have breakfast with us.

CORA

We had breakfast at the depot.

VINNIE

Well, as a matter of fact, we'd just finished.

FATHER

[*with cold dignity*] *I* haven't finished my breakfast!

VINNIE

Well, then sit down, Clare. [*to* CORA *and* MARY] Margaret gave us kippers this morning and Clare's so fond of kippers. Why don't we all sit down? [*indicates the empty places and the girls sit.* FATHER *resumes his chair and breakfast in stony silence.* MAGGIE *has come into the room to await orders.*] Maggie, clear those things away. [*she indicates the dishes in front of the girls, and* MAGGIE *removes them.* FATHER *takes a letter from his stack of morning mail and opens it.*] Clare, don't let your kippers get cold. [*to* CORA] Now — tell us all about Springfield.

CORA

We had a wonderful month — but tell us about you, Cousin Vinnie. You must have had a terrible time.

VINNIE

Yes, I was pretty sick, but I'm all right again now.

CORA

What was it?

VINNIE

Well, the doctors don't know exactly, but they did say this — that they'd never seen anything like it before, whatever it was.

CORA

You certainly look well enough now. Doesn't she, Clare?

> [*Whatever is in the letter* FATHER *has been reading comes to him as a shock.*]

FATHER

Oh, God!

VINNIE

What's the matter, Clare? What's wrong?

FATHER

John! John!

> [JOHN *is seen halfway up the stairs with the girls' bags. He comes running down the stairs, going to* FATHER.]

JOHN

Yes, Father?

FATHER

Have you been going around this town selling medicine?

JOHN

[*a little frightened*] Yes, Father.

FATHER

Dog medicine?

JOHN

[*indignantly*] No, Father, not dog medicine!

FATHER

It must have been dog medicine!

JOHN

It wasn't dog medicine, Father —

FATHER

This letter from Mrs. Sprague says you sold her a
bottle of this medicine and that her little boy gave some
of it to their dog and it killed him! Now she wants ten
dollars from me for a new dog.

JOHN

Well, he shouldn't have given it to a dog. It's for hu-
mans! Why, it's Bartlett's Beneficent Balm — "Made
from a secret formula"!

FATHER

Have you been going around among our friends and
neighbors selling some damned Dr. Munyon patent nos-
trum?

JOHN

But it's good medicine, Father. I can prove it by Mother.

FATHER

Vinnie, what do you know about this?

VINNIE

Nothing, Clare, but I'm sure that John —

JOHN

No, I mean that day Mother —

FATHER

That's enough! You're going to every house where you sold a bottle of that concoction and buy it all back.

JOHN

[*dismayed*] But it's a dollar a bottle!

FATHER

I don't care how much it is. How many bottles did you sell?

JOHN

A hundred and twenty-eight.

FATHER

[*roaring*] A hundred and twenty-eight!

VINNIE

Clare, I always told you John would make a good business man.

FATHER

[*calmly*] Young man, I'll give you the money to buy it back — a hundred and twenty-eight dollars. And ten more for Mrs. Sprague. That's a hundred and thirty-eight dollars. But it's coming out of your allowance! That means you'll not get another penny until that hundred and thirty-eight dollars is all paid up.

> [J O H N *starts toward the hall, counting on his fingers, then turns and addresses his father in dismay.*]

JOHN

I'll be twenty-one years old!

> [F A T H E R *glares at him.* J O H N *turns and goes on up the stairs, with the bags.*]

VINNIE

[*persuasively*] Clare, you know you've always encouraged the boys to earn their own money.

FATHER

Vinnie, I'll handle this. [*there is a pause. He buries himself in his newspaper.*]

CORA

[*breaking through the constraint*] Of course, Aunt Judith sent her love to all of you —

VINNIE

I haven't seen Judith for years. You'd think living so close to Springfield — maybe I could run up there before the summer's over.

CORA

Oh, she'll be leaving for Pleasantville any day now. Grandpa Ebbetts has been failing very fast and that's why I have to hurry back.

VINNIE

Hurry back? Well, you and Mary can stay with us a few days at least.

CORA

No, I hate to break the news to you, Vinnie, but we can't even stay overnight. We're leaving on the five o'clock train this afternoon.

VINNIE

[*disappointed*] Oh, what a pity!

[FATHER *lowers the paper.*]

FATHER

[*heartily*] Well, Cora, it certainly is good to see you again. [*to* MARY] Young lady, I think you've been enjoying yourself — you look prettier than ever.

[MARY *laughs and blushes.*]

WHITNEY

I'll bet Clarence will think so.

[*The doorbell rings.* MAGGIE *crosses to answer it.*]

FATHER

That can't be another special delivery for Clarence. [*to* MARY, *slyly*] While you were in Springfield our postman was kept pretty busy. Sure you girls don't want any breakfast?

MARY

No, thank you. [*rises and goes to the arch and stands looking upstairs, watching for* CLARENCE.]

CORA

Oh, no, thank you, Cousin Clare, we've had our breakfast.

FATHER

At least you ought to have a cup of coffee with us. Vinnie, you might have thought to order some coffee for the girls.

CORA

No, no, thank you, Cousin Clare.

[MAGGIE *appears again in the arch.*]

MAGGIE

It's the cab, ma'am. [*exits.*]

FATHER

The cab! What cab?

VINNIE

The cab that's to take us to Audubon.

FATHER

Who's going to Audubon?

VINNIE

We all are. Cora, the most wonderful thing has happened!

CORA

What, Cousin Vinnie?

VINNIE

[*happily*] Clare's going to be baptized this morning.

FATHER

[*not believing his ears*] Vinnie — what are you saying?

VINNIE

[*with determination*] I'm saying you're going to be baptized this morning!

FATHER

I am not going to be baptized this morning or any other morning!

VINNIE

You promised yesterday that as soon as I sent that pug dog back you'd be baptized.

FATHER

I promised no such thing!

VINNIE

You certainly did!

FATHER

I never said anything remotely like that!

VINNIE

Clarence was right here and heard it. You ask him!

FATHER

Clarence be damned! I know what I said! I don't remember exactly, but it wasn't that!

VINNIE

Well, I remember. That's why I ordered the cab!

FATHER

[*suddenly remembering*] The cab! Oh, my God, that cab! [*he rises and glares out the window at the cab, then turns back and speaks peremptorily.*] Vinnie! You send that right back!

VINNIE

I'll do nothing of the kind. I'm going to see that you get to Heaven.

FATHER

I can't go to Heaven in a cab!

VINNIE

Well, you can start in a cab! I'm not sure whether they'll ever let you into Heaven or not, but I know they won't unless you're baptized.

FATHER

They can't keep me out of Heaven on a technicality.

VINNIE

Clare, stop quibbling! You might as well face it —
you've got to make your peace with God.

FATHER

I never had any trouble with God until you stirred Him
up!

[MARY *is tired of waiting for* CLAR-
ENCE *and chooses this moment to inter-
rupt.*]

MARY

Mrs. Day?

[VINNIE *answers her quickly, as if expecting* MARY *to supply her with an
added argument.*]

VINNIE

Yes, Mary?

MARY

Where do you suppose Clarence is?

FATHER

You keep out of this, young lady! If it hadn't been for
you, no one would have known whether I was baptized
or not.

[MARY *breaks into tears.*]

Damn! Damnation!

VINNIE

Harlan! Whitney! Get your Sunday hats. [*calls up-stairs*] John! Clarence!

> [HARLAN *and* WHITNEY *start out,*
> *but stop as* FATHER *speaks.*]

FATHER

[*blazing with new fire*] Vinnie, are you mad? Was it your plan that my own children should witness this indignity?

VINNIE

Why, Clare, they'll be proud of you!

FATHER

I suppose Harlan is to be my godfather! [*with determination*] Vinnie, it's no use. I can't go through with this thing and I won't. That's final.

VINNIE

Why, Clare dear, if you feel that way about it —

FATHER

I do!

VINNIE

— the children don't have to go.

> [JOHN *enters.*]

JOHN

Yes, Mother?

ACT III SCENE II

Clarence comes down the steps in his new suit . . . without saying a word he kneels in front of her.

[F A T H E R *sees* J O H N *and an avenue of escape opens up.*]

FATHER

Oh, John! Vinnie, I can't do anything like that this morning. I've got to take John down to the office and give him the money to buy back that medicine. [*to* J O H N] When I think of you going around this town selling dog medicine!—

JOHN

[*insistently*] It wasn't dog medicine, Father.

FATHER

John, we're starting downtown this minute!

VINNIE

You're doing no such thing! You gave me your Sacred Promise that day I almost died—

JOHN

Yes, and she would have died if we hadn't given her some of that medicine. That proves it's good medicine!

FATHER

[*aghast*] You gave your mother some of that dog medicine!

VINNIE

Oh, no, John, you didn't! [*sinks weakly into the chair below the fireplace.*]

JOHN

Yes, we did, Mother. We put some in your tea that morning.

FATHER

You did what? Without her knowing it? Do you realize you might have killed your mother? You did kill Mrs. Sprague's dog. [*after a solemn pause*] John, you've done a very serious thing. I'll have to give considerable thought as to how you're going to be punished for this.

VINNIE

But, Clare—

FATHER

No, Vinnie. When I think of that day — with the house full of doctors — why, Cora, we even sent for the minister. Why, we might have lost you! [*he goes to* VINNIE, *really moved, and puts his hand on her shoulder.*] It's all right now, Vinnie, thank God. You're well again. But what I went through that afternoon — the way I felt — I'll never forget it.

VINNIE

Don't talk that way, Clare. You've forgotten it already.

FATHER

What do you mean?

VINNIE

That was the day you gave me your Sacred Promise.

FATHER

But I wouldn't have promised if I hadn't thought you were dying — and you wouldn't have almost died if John hadn't given you that medicine. Don't you see? The whole thing's illegal!

VINNIE

Suppose I had died! It wouldn't make any difference to you. You don't care whether we meet in Heaven or not — you don't care whether you ever see me and the children again.

> [*She almost succeeds in crying.* HAR-LAN *and* WHITNEY *go to her in sympathy, putting their arms around her.*]

FATHER

[*distressed*] Now, Vinnie, you're not being fair to me.

VINNIE

It's all right, Clare. If you don't love us enough there's nothing we can do about it.

> [*Hurt,* FATHER *walks away to the other side of the room.*]

FATHER

That's got nothing to do with it! I love my family as much as any man. There's nothing within reason I wouldn't do for you, and you know it! All these years I've struggled and worked just to prove — [*he has reached the window and looks out.*] There's that damn cab! Vinnie, you're not well enough to go all the way up to Audubon.

VINNIE

[*perkily*] I'm well enough if we ride.

FATHER

But that trip would take all morning. And those cabs cost a dollar an hour.

VINNIE

[*with smug complacence*] That's one of their best cabs. That costs two dollars an hour.

> [FATHER *stares at her a second, horri-
> fied — then explodes.*]

FATHER

Then why aren't you ready? Get your hat on! Damn! Damnation! Amen! [*exits for his hat and stick.* VIN-NIE *is stunned for a moment by this sudden surrender, then hastily puts on her bonnet.*]

WHITNEY

Let's watch them start! Come on, Cousin Cora, let's watch them start!

CORA

I wouldn't miss it!

> [WHITNEY, HARLAN, *and* CORA
> *hurry out.* VINNIE *starts, but* JOHN
> *stops her in the arch.*]

ACT III SCENE II

FATHER

"No! I'm going to be baptized, damn it."

JOHN

[*contritely*] Mother, I didn't mean to almost kill you.

VINNIE

Now, don't you worry about what your father said. [*tenderly*] It's all right, dear. [*she kisses him.*] It worked out fine! [*she exits.* JOHN *looks upstairs, then at* MARY, *who has gone to the window.*]

JOHN

Mary! Here comes Clarence!

[JOHN *exits.* MARY *sits in* FATHER'S *chair.* CLARENCE *comes down the stairs in his new suit. He goes into the room and right to* MARY. *Without saying a word he kneels in front of her. They both are starry-eyed.*]
[FATHER, *with hat and stick, comes into the arch on his way out. He sees* CLARENCE *kneeling at* MARY'S *feet.*]

FATHER

Oh, God!

[CLARENCE *springs up in embarrassment.* VINNIE *re-enters hurriedly.*]

VINNIE

What's the matter? What's wrong?

CLARENCE

Nothing's wrong, Mother — [*then, for want of some-thing to say*] Going to the office, Father?

FATHER

No! I'm going to be baptized, damn it!

> [*He slams his hat on angrily and stalks out.* VINNIE *gives a triumphant nod and follows him. The curtain starts down, and as it falls,* CLARENCE *again kneels at* MARY'S *feet.*]

CURTAIN